Peer Gynt

HENRIK IBSEN

Peer Gynt

TRANSLATED BY GERRY BAMMAN
AND IRENE B. BERMAN

TCG TRANSLATIONS

Peer Gynt is published by Theatre Communications Group, Inc., 355 Lexington Ave., New York, NY 10017.

TCG gratefully acknowledges public funds from the National Endowment for the Arts, the New York State Council on the Arts and the New York City Department of Cultural Affairs in addition to the generous support of the following foundations and corporations: Alcoa Foundation, Ameritech Foundation, ARCO Foundation, AT&T Foundation, Consolidated Edison Company of New York, Council of Literary Magazines and Presses, Nathan Cummings Foundation, Dayton Hudson Foundation, Ford Foundation, GTE, James Irvine Foundation, Jerome Foundation, Management Consultants for the Arts, Andrew W. Mellon Foundation, Metropolitan Life Foundation, National Broadcasting Company, Pew Charitable Trusts, Philip Morris Companies Inc., Scherman Foundation, Shubert Foundation, L. J. Skaggs and Mary C. Skaggs Foundation, Lila Wallace-Reader's Digest Fund.

Ibsen, Henrik, 1828-1906
[Peer Gynt. English]
Peer Gynt / Henrik Ibsen : translated by Gerry Bamman and Irene B. Berman.
—1st ed.
(TCG Translations 2)
Translation of: Peer Gynt.
ISBN 1-55936-046-1 (cloth)—ISBN 1-55936-045-3 (paper)
I. Bamman, Gerry. II. Berman, Irene B. III. Title. IV. Series.
PT8876.A323 1992
839.8'226—dc20   92-2564
                                                              CIP

Cover design and watercolor copyright © 1992 by Barry Moser
Design and composition by The Sarabande Press
Color separations provided by EMR Systems Communication

First Edition, July 1992

ACKNOWLEDGMENTS

The world premiere of this translation of *Peer Gynt* was produced at the Hartford Stage Company, Hartford, Connecticut, Mark Lamos, Artistic Director.

The translators would like to thank Martin M. Berman, M.D.; Tor Guttu, lexicographer, University of Oslo; Joanne Kurnik, Accent, Inc.; Mark Lamos, Greg Leaming and the staff of the Hartford Stage Company; and Richard Thomas.

Special thanks to a close nucleus of Norwegian friends living in the United States who constantly help keep Norwegian culture and traditions alive, and who have contributed to the challenge of understanding the nuances of Henrik Ibsen and of rendering them into correct English; and to Runa, Kaare and Bard for their support while doing research for this project.

CONTENTS

Introduction
by Gerry Bamman and Irene B. Berman
ix

Peer Gynt
I

Introduction

The process of translation involves seemingly never-ending choices. The same suit of clothes that fit so comfortably on that gentleman in Oslo looks a little out of place on the fellow now trying to wear the same outfit in Topeka—particularly when it has been handed down through several generations. A few alterations will make it look better, and that is where the choices begin. Was that collar meant to look frayed, or has it just been worn through by so many people using it? Was he never wearing a belt, or has it been lost? The theatre, moreover, presents particular problems for the translator. The characters often speak in every-day language—idioms, slang and colloquial speech—that is difficult to find equivalents for in another language, and that is so awash in innuendo and extra-literal meaning that it is almost impossible for a nonnative to understand completely. A character in an American play need only say a few words before an American audience can begin to construct his geographical, educational and ethnic background. That instant recognition, however, rarely happens when a translation is involved—be it of Ibsen, Chekhov or any other playwright. This is due in part to the audience's lack of familiarity with the clues that are given.

When reading *Peer Gynt*, for example, a Norwegian would bring an awareness of trolls to the play that would be very different from the perception of an American, who would tend to picture them as cute and fuzzy. A Norwegian would know that trolls are supernatural creatures who steal from human beings. In appearance, they are distorted humans: they might, for example, have one eye or several heads; they can be larger or smaller than men; and there are mountain trolls, forest trolls and ocean trolls. They are all menacing to humans but—mercifully—not very bright; in a confrontation between a troll and a human, the good human will emerge victorious. To a Norwegian child, trolls are as much a part of the environment as food on the table or fresh air, and children are never quite sure that one may not materialize in front of them. They are a constant challenge to be on one's good behavior and to use one's intelligence; otherwise, the troll will overpower you and carry you off. In everyday Norwegian, "troll" can be used as a predicate. For example, "Don't be trolly" would mean "Don't be bad." Or, "He is a real troll"—he is not a good man, he is a monster.

Ibsen adds a symbolic layer to the folklore concept. His trolls are usually gnomic in stature, and they appear at times of crisis and threaten the mortal and emotional stability of humans. Peer Gynt is saved by church bells or religious connections that are not an integral part of the folklore. The menace, however, is real as well as symbolic, and is not to be taken lightly. A translator has limited powers to convey such different cultural contexts as this because they are often nontextual.

A translator can help an audience, however, to pick up an author's clues by avoiding the sanitization that often occurs in transferring a word from one language to another. Grammatical errors, for example, that the author puts into the character's mouth in order to make a point should not be corrected in English. If a character uses a word that is surprising—for example, if someone were to drop "copacetic" into the middle of a conversation, revealing something about his or her personality—that word cannot then be toned down to "fine" or "satisfactory" in the translation.

Like the journalist, who reports on events to an audience who usually were not present and have no access to the actual scene, a translator presents material to an audience who by and large have no access to the original language. Both the journalist and the translator would like to think of themselves as objective, their choices unbiased and empirical. In fact, however, that is not the case. The choices made are informed by certain assumptions, personality traits, prejudices and predilections, many of which cannot even be articulated. But insofar as they can be discovered, we feel bound to do so in order to give the reader an idea of our point of view.

The first and most obvious decision was to translate *Peer Gynt* into rhyming verse, attempting to match the form of the Norwegian. There are a number of prose translations, but few in verse. Not only is verse more difficult, but one must necessarily make some compromises in accuracy—more than one would in translating the prose plays, for example. It is our hope, however, that a verse translation of a verse play presents a truer rendering than a prose version which is more faithful to the words themselves—an arguable choice, perhaps, but one which the reader can evaluate by comparison.

Ibsen was rather idiosyncratic in the styles of verse that he employed, varying the rhyme scheme and meter to suit his purposes from scene to scene and speech to speech. We have followed his example, employing a shorter, more comic line in some scenes—for instance, those with Anitra—and a longer, more lyrical line in others—for example, the death of Aase (in which Ibsen is at his most formal, even alternating masculine and feminine rhymes). We have not used as many end-stopped couplets as Ibsen because we found in production that the effect was less than felicitous. This could be due to a difference in the languages, in the sensibilities of the respective audiences, or to the indisputable fact that Ibsen was a better poet and more able to make such devices work.

Otherwise, we have tried to follow Ibsen's rhyme scheme as much as possible. For example, an examination of the first fourteen lines of the play reveals the following pattern: ABABC-CDEEDFGFG. We have the same scheme in our version. The next twenty-two lines in Ibsen are a bit more capricious: AB-BACBDCEEDDFFGHGIJJHI. We wove a variation in English as follows: ABBACBDCEEDFDFGGHIJJHI. Alterations were undertaken only to improve fidelity to the meaning of the original lines, or to improve the sound of the English verse. We attempted to be faithful without being fanatical. When the bed was too short, we altered the bed rather than the sleeper.

Another major premise upon which we have based our translations is our refusal to try to recreate Victorian or nineteenth-century dialogue. It is, again, an arguable choice, because the case could be made that one should try to duplicate the sound of the era in which the play was written. Our main objection, however, is that neither we nor anyone else alive today can say for certain what that sound was, and it is, therefore, a theoretical exercise that cannot be verified. We have in all cases tried to avoid any vocabulary that is not known to have been extant in the nineteenth century. It is our hope that we have arrived at a mode of speech that is comfortable—even familiar—to contemporary ears without anachronisms that would create confusion. When we have employed slang (of nineteenth-century vintage only), it is to match Ibsen's usage, not an attempt to make the dialogue more "modern." On the other hand, when Ibsen has employed a more formal vocabulary or mode of expression, we have tried to find an equivalent. One of the clearest examples would be the numerous occasions in *Peer Gynt* when a character—most often the Old Man of Dovre—resorts to an archaic use of the verb "to be." To convey that shift, we have used the Biblical "thou art" and variations.

A particularly nettlesome problem to resolve is the number of expressions from the play that have entered the Norwegian language and have become quite colloquial, liable to pop up in anyone's conversation, just as "Neither a borrower nor a lender be" and many other Shakespearean lines have done in English. To translate them literally would give no sense of that familiarity. When Peer says—in our version—"Whether I will, whether I won't / Damned if I do, damned if I don't," he is using a phrase that has become a familiar part of everyday Norwegian speech that has a similar meaning but would more literally be translated as, "Everyone complains just as much whether I'm hammered or I do the hammering." It's not unintelligible in English, by any means, but we chose to use an expression that would convey how familiar the words have become to a Norwegian.

We were not, however, always able to find such an equivalent. In Act IV, for example, when Peer has been made a fool of by Anitra, he ends his monologue with a line that has become familiar to every Norwegian, which literally says, "And women—as a species, they aren't worth much." We were not able to land upon a phrase that would be a similar conversational "button" as it is in Norwegian, and still remain true to the intent of the original. We hope our version retains the humor, however:

I'd like to spare you all the sordid detail
But!—Modern man's a hypocrite and petty—
Hearts without wings, deeds without weight—and yet he
Is a damn sight better than your modern female!

All non-Norwegian words and expressions—German, Italian, French, etc.—have been left in the text as Ibsen wrote them. We assume that if he wished them to be untranslated for Norwegians, he would want the same for an English-speaking audience.

Puns present another dilemma, for it is rare that the literal words will play the same in the second language as they do in the first. An example is the passage in Act I, Scene i, in which Aase speaks of her husband—in our version—as "well-heeled Jon" who "took to his heels in shame." The original makes a play on words between "Jon with the money bags" who "took off with his peddler's sack"; which, unfortunately, English does not allow us to do. We chose, therefore, to keep the pun and the spirit of the pun rather than the literal meaning.

Each Ibsen play has one or two particularly vexing problems for the translator. In *Hedda Gabler* it is Tesman's verbal tic, "Hva", with which he ends a sentence or a statement over eighty times in the play. In *A Doll House*, it is Nora's word "the wonderful," with which she describes again and again her hopes for rescue. In *Peer Gynt*, one of the two challenges was the troll motto versus the human motto, first articulated by the Old Man of Dovre. Literally, those words are "Be yourself" versus "Be yourself—enough." They are quite cryptic and mysterious even in Norwegian, but the human motto has a positive innuendo, and the troll motto a negative one. Still, it is innuendo; it is not spelled out. It is with trepidation, then, that we follow William Archer's lead and translate "Be yourself" as "To thine own self be true," because it does seem that we are explicating and expanding on the original. Our fear, however, was that the more literal translation would be too murky for an English-speaking audience who do not have the familiarity with the play that the Norwegians do. The advantage gained, on the other hand, in using the Shakespearean line is the increased understanding, along with the undeniably positive reverberations, the aura of gentle moral suasion. Then that notion is thrown just a bit askew by the trolls adding "enough." Enough to serve yourself, enough to get away with.

The second challenge in *Peer Gynt* is the Boyg. All versions in English with which we are familiar—unlike those we have seen in French and German—have left the name untranslated. We feel that is a mistake since the word is not just a proper name in

Norwegian but means "the bent one." In Norwegian folklore, the Boyg is an invisible, gigantic creature in the shape of a large snake. In *Peer Gynt*, the Boyg is thought by most interpreters to be the embodiment of the spirit of compromise, or a symbol of Peer's lack of will. In most normal usage, the Boyg has come to represent the obstacles between a person and his or her fulfillment. In English, we do not have the folklore monster, but in an effort to retain some of the symbolism while using a comprehensible word, we have named him the Great Between.

Finally, let us say a few words on the subject of profanity. Each language has its own version of the profane; the Norwegian is no exception. The worst oaths a Norwegian can utter have to do with hell and the devil. "Black devil" would arouse little interest here, but would be shocking and offensive in Norway. It is the social ripple that a word or phrase would cause that seems to us the key, not whether that word is literally translated. Let's look at the first two examples in the play. In Act I, Scene i, Aase says to Peer, "Christ on the cross, how you can talk!" "Christ on the cross" would be literally translated as "cross on cross" and is a mild oath. The change is only to turn it into a profanity that makes some sense to our audience's ears. In Act I, Scene ii, Peer says to Aslak, "What the hell do you want?" More literally it would be "What the devil"—again a mild oath (not the same word as the afore-mentioned "black devil"; it is a more formal and gentler version). We have changed devil to hell because, to our ears, devil has character implications that are not warranted here.

It is our hope that the foregoing will help shed some light on our version of the text. Translations are prisms through which one looks at the original—they are not the original itself. Although we have Ibsen's text to guide us, we do not have Ibsen. By citing these specific examples, we hope the reader may better understand the medium through which he is looking at Mr. Ibsen and *Peer Gynt*.

                                        —*Gerry Bamman and Irene B. Berman*

Peer Gynt

CHARACTERS

Aase, a farmer's widow.
Peer Gynt, her son.
Two old crones carrying sacks of grain.
Aslak, a blacksmith.
Wedding guests. The Master of Ceremonies. Fiddler, etc.
A couple of new people in town.
Solveig and little Helga, their daughters.
The farmer at Haegstad.
Ingrid, his daughter.
The groom and his parents.
Three herd girls.
A woman dressed in green.
The Old Man of Dovre.
A court troll. Several like him.
Troll girls and troll children.
A couple of witches.
Troll people, gnomes, goblins, etc.

An ugly kid. A voice in the darkness. Bird calls.

Kari, a cotter's wife.

Master Cotton, Monsieur Ballon, Messrs. von Eberkopf and
    Trumpeterstraale, traveling salesmen.

A thief and a fence.

Anitra, the daughter of the Bedouin chief.

Arabs, slave girls, dancing girls, etc.

The Memnon statue (singing).

The Sphinx at Gizeh (a mute).

Professor Begriffenfeldt, Ph.D., director of the madhouse in Cairo.

Huhu, a linguistics teacher from the Malabar Coast.

Hussein, an Oriental politician.

A Fellah with a royal mummy.

Several inmates of the madhouse and their guardians.

A Norwegian skipper and his crew.

A strange passenger.

A minister.

A funeral procession.

A sheriff.

A button molder.

A scrawny person.

The play begins at the turn of this century[1] and ends around our
own time, taking place in Gudbrandsdalen[2] and the high mountains
nearby, on the coast of Morocco, in the Sahara Desert, in the mad-
house in Cairo, at sea, etc.

Act One

A wooded hillside near Aase's farm. A river runs downhill. An old mill on the other side. A hot summer day.

    Peer Gynt, a solidly built twenty-year-old boy, comes down the footpath. Aase, his mother, pert and trim, follows after him. She is ill tempered and screaming.

AASE:
    Peer,[3] you're a liar!

PEER GYNT *(Without stopping)*:
                No, I'm not!

AASE:
    Then swear it's true—look in my eyes!

PEER GYNT:
    Why should I swear?

AASE:
                Just what I thought!
    Nothing but lies—hot air and lies!

PEER GYNT *(Stops)*:
    I tell you—every blessed word is true!

AASE *(Facing him)*:

>   For shame! Do you know who you're talking to?
>   You run away for months on end
>   Deer hunting in the mountains, in the season
>   I need you most—the harvest! And what's the reason
>   For your return? So I can mend
>   The coat you've torn. You have no game.
>   You've lost your gun. And without blinking
>   You tell a story that would shame
>   A fisherman. What are you thinking?
>   Now where is it you ran into this buck?

PEER GYNT:

>   A little west of Gjendin.[4]

AASE *(Laughs sarcastically)*:

>   Oh, I see!

PEER GYNT:

>   The wind was swirling, blowing bitterly—
>   Hidden behind a grove of trees, he struck
>   His hoof against the snowy ground—once, twice—
>   Looking for lichen—

AASE *(As before)*:

>   Yes, of course, what luck!

PEER GYNT:

>   I held my breath, and stood stock still.
>   I heard his hoof squeak against the ice,
>   And I could see his antlers branching high
>   Above my head—seeming to scratch the sky.
>   I fell upon my stomach, inched uphill,
>   Hidden among the rocks; so shiny,
>   So fat a buck—mother, it was a thrill
>   To see him! Even I felt tiny!

AASE:

>   Oh, goodness me!

PEER GYNT:

Bang! At the sound
Of my gun, the buck falls to the ground.
And in the quarter-second that he's down
I leap across his heaving back,
I grab his ear and hold on for dear life,
I'm poised and just about to plunge my knife
Into his neck below his antlered crown
When hey! The monster screams, and crack!
He scrambles to all fours, and in a flash
I'm flying backwards as he spins
And leaps. My knife and sheath go flying and crash
Against the ice; and then he pins
Me—helpless, terrified—by the thigh
Against his flank—with horns like giant tongs
He squeezes me, then bolts toward clear, blue sky
And Gjendin ridge, as if that will right the wrongs
I've done him.

AASE *(Despite herself)*:

Good Lord—

PEER GYNT:

Did you ever see
The Gjendin ridge? Its length? Its height?
It's more than three miles long, and right
Atop the crest, sharper than a razor's edge,
You're looking down past glaciers, past the scree,
Past many a barren, icy mountain ledge,
And on both sides simultaneously
You see the sleepy water billow
Black, heavy, maybe two or three
Miles down—a distant, deadly pillow.
Along that ridge, he and I
Blazed like a comet through the sky.

I've ridden many mounts, but never one
Like this. It seemed to me the course
He ran would lead us straight into the sun.
But halfway down, a dizzy force
Beckoned—brown backs of eagles floated
Languorously, almost invitingly,
As we sped overhead unnoted.
Farther down I could see ice floes cracking, see
The shoreline trembling—not a sound was heard.
Like dancers, the spirits of the waves
Were luring us to watery graves
With kicks and twirls, not uttering a word.

AASE *(Dizzy)*:

Oh, God help me!

PEER GYNT:

        Then, mother dear,
Above a cliff hopelessly sheer
A grouse to which we gave a scare
Trembled and fluttered, then it flapped and beat
Its wings between the buck's front feet,
And—shrieking—soared into the air.
The buck shied back, turned halfway round,
Bounded high, high above the ground
And off the edge to certain suicide.

(Aase staggers and grabs hold of a tree trunk. Peer Gynt continues)

Above—the black walls of the mountainside;
Beneath—is nothing but the atmosphere.
We cut through fog—it's quiet, peaceful—
And then we pass a gliding seagull
Who flaps off with a frenzied cry,
Causing his mates to screech and fly
Away. Down, down goes the strange procession,

But far below is a faint impression
Of something white—the belly of a deer!
Our own reflection—the buck and me!—
Careening through the quiet sea
At the same wild speed that we come down—
Rushing to greet us at the ocean's crust
To tell us we will surely drown!

AASE *(Gasping for air)*:

God! Then what happened? Tell me! Peer!

PEER GYNT:

I'm just
About to! Buck from air and buck from sea
Butted their heads simultaneously.
Spume and foam flew around us—one wave crashing
Against another—we were splashing, thrashing!
Minutes, or hours later—maybe more,
I don't know now—we reached the northern shore.
The buck did all the swimming—I held on.
Then I came home.

AASE:

But what about the buck?
Tell me!

PEER GYNT:

Oh, mother, I think he's long gone.

(Snaps his fingers, turns on his heel, and adds)

If you can find him, he's all yours! Good luck!

AASE:

Oh, Peer, you haven't broken something, have you?
And where he crushed you—how's your thigh?
Your head's intact? My pride, my joy!
Oh, praise and thanks to God on high
Who deigned to help my little boy!

His pants are torn and need attention
But Lord, that's scarcely worth a mention
Considering what a beast like that could do!
A tale like that would horrify—

(Suddenly stops, looks at him wide-eyed and open-mouthed; no words come; finally she exclaims)

You devil, you! More and more lies!
Christ on the cross, how you can talk!
Do you think I can't recognize
This string of whoppers? I heard all
Of this when I could barely walk!
It's Gudbrand Glesne[5] took this fall,
Not you—!

PEER GYNT:

          It happened to me, too,
Mother! These things can happen more than once!

AASE *(Angry)*:

A lie can be turned inside out
So it's unrecognizable—all you
Must do is change it all about
So it can't be identified! You dunce,
I know your mind, your little machinations.
You dress things up with wild exaggerations,
You flesh the story out with grouse
And eagles and anything else a souse
Can conjure! Without the slightest shame,
You lie till odd and even seem the same,
And hope that in the end I won't recall
I've heard this lie before—yes, heard it all!

PEER GYNT:

Mother, if anybody else had said
What you just said, I'd give him such

A beating!

AASE *(Crying)*:

God, I wish that I were dead!
I wish that I were in the ground!
My prayers don't touch you, tears don't touch
You; Peer, you're lost! You should have drowned!

PEER GYNT:

Sweet, little mother, look at me—please do—
Every single word you say is true.
Now please, my dear, be happy—

AASE:

Quiet!
My son's a pig who's running riot—
What in the world is there to make me happy?
You want me to feel better? Stop heaping
Shame on me! Look, I'm old—barely keeping
Myself alive. Help me, Peer—and make it snappy!

(Cries again)

Look at us—not a cent is left
Of father's money! Bushels of coins passed on
To him by Rasmus Gynt—where are they?—Gone!
Gone with the wind! Now we're bereft!
Oh, when I think of how it ran
Right through your father's fingers. That man
Kept buying land in every single county,
Rode around in golden wagons! And the bounty
Wasted at Christmas time on feasts
For all his friends—the stupid beasts!—
Who smashed our finest crystal, all
In drunken fun, against the wall!

PEER GYNT:

Yes, yes—where are the snows of yesteryear?

AASE:

    Be quiet when your mother's speaking, hear?
    Look at the farm! The doorframe sags,
    Our windowpanes are bedspreads—rags!
    Fences and gates are falling down,
    Cattle and sheep are lost, or drown
    From inattention! Fields—worn out!
    Each month I borrow more and more—

PEER GYNT:

    What's this old woman's talk about!
    Bad luck has come and gone before
    And you've recovered, haven't you?

AASE:

    Salt has been sown where our luck grew.
    But you think you're so great—Oh, right! He
    Stands there so smug and high-and-mighty,
    As smug as when the minister
    From Copenhagen asked him what
    His baptized name was, sinister
    Old stinkpot that he was; he got
    Your father to present him with a horse
    And sleigh because he said, "That boy
    Has brains a king or viceroy
    Would envy"! We had friends then—yes, of course!
    The minister, the captain—all
    Would hang around day in, day out,
    Eating until they were about
    To burst. But once you take a fall—
    Oh, they don't even know your name.
    The visitors were all long gone
    The very day that "well-heeled Jon"
    Went bust and took to his heels in shame.

(She dries her eyes with her apron)

Peer, you're the one who's big and strong—
You should support me—be my staff
As I grow feeble and along
In years—and care for the farm—one half
Of it is yours—all of it when I die!

(She cries again)

"She gave the farm," my epitaph
Will say, "To Peer, and he gave her a lie."
When you sit staring at the fireplace,
Stirring the embers, you think you're working!
You irk the villagers by smirking
About kissing their girls behind the staircase!
You'll fight anyone, anywhere!
You shame me here—you shame me there—

PEER GYNT *(Leaving her)*:

Leave me alone.

AASE *(Following him)*:

                  Do you dispute
That you were the first to enter the melee
At Lunde? First, a little grog
And then gleefully you join the fray!
One drink and you're a rabid dog!
You're proud of acting like a brute!
You break the blacksmith's arm, and dislocate
His finger, and you think you're cute!
But I'm the one that you humiliate!

PEER GYNT:

You're wrong, you know. It wasn't what it seemed!

AASE *(Fuming)*:

Come on! Kari heard Aslak when he screamed!

PEER GYNT *(Rubbing his elbow)*:
>   But I'm the one who screamed. You've been misled.

AASE:
>   Not you!

PEER GYNT:
>   Yes, mother—get it through your head!

AASE:
>   What's that? What's that?

PEER GYNT:
>   Mother, he's strong.

AASE:
>   Who's strong? Who's strong?

PEER GYNT:
>   Aslak is strong, I said!

AASE:
>   Phooey! And phooey twice! I spit
>   On you! That drunkard! That nitwit!
>   That cockeyed boozer? That pubcrawler
>   Has beaten you and made you holler?

>   *(Cries again)*

>   You've done me great disgrace and wrong,
>   But this? Peer, this I have to call
>   The low point—it's the worst of all.
>   He's strong—so what? That makes you weak?
>   If he is bold, must you be meek?

PEER GYNT:
>   Whether I will, whether I won't,
>   Damned if I do—damned if I don't!

>   *(Laughs)*

>   Calm down—

AASE:

Is this another of your lies?
Peer! Not again!

PEER GYNT:

I lied, but it's the first
And only time. Don't cry now. Dry your eyes.

(Makes a fist with his left hand)

Look! With these pliers I immobilize
The smith, and beat him into liverwurst
With this—my hammer—my right fist—

AASE:

You thug! You hoodlum! Anarchist!
You're going to put me in my grave!

PEER GYNT:

No, don't! I promise I'll behave
Better—a thousand times better! Don't cry,
Sweet, little, nasty mother, take
My word. I'll change my ways. I'll make
You proud of me, you'll see! Wait till I
Do something—something really big! The town
Will honor you and bask in your renown.

AASE *(Blows in contempt)*:

Sure!

PEER GYNT:

Mother, you'll see! I'm newborn!

AASE:

If you possessed the skill and pride
To mend your pants when you have torn
Them brawling, I'd be satisfied.

PEER GYNT *(Angrily)*:

I will be king! Emperor!

AASE:

    God! Should I lose my temper or
    Drop dead from shame. You've lost what little wit
    You had.

PEER GYNT:

                I'll do it if you'll wait a bit!

AASE:

    Really! Who died and made you king
    Are words with a familiar ring!

PEER GYNT:

    I'll do it, mother!

AASE:

              Hold your tongue!
    You're off your rocker! You're unstrung!
    You could do something—yes, of course—
    And even something big, God knows!—well, maybe—
    But not by spending every day with lazy
    Louts drinking and bragging yourself hoarse.
    You know quite well that Haegstad girl was crazy
    For you. You could have played that game and won
    If you had wanted. Now your chance is gone—

PEER GYNT:

    Ingrid? I could have got her?

AASE:

              That old man
    Haegstad would never contradict the girl.
    He would love to have the final say,
    Of course, but once his precious little pearl
    Makes up her mind, she goes her way,
    With him following along as best he can.

(Starts to cry again)

    A wealthy girl! The match was heaven-sent.

Imagine, Peer! You would have got their farm.
All that you would have had to do was flirt
With her, and you'd be walking arm in arm
Today, not standing here in rags and dirt.

PEER GYNT *(Quickly)*:

Mother, come! Let's go get his consent!

AASE:

Where are you going?

PEER GYNT:

Haegstad!

AASE:

You poor thing!
You're just a little late, considering . . .

PEER GYNT:

What?

AASE:

Oh, my God, all I can do is sigh!
You've wasted time and opportunity—

PEER GYNT:

But—

AASE *(Sobbing)*:

Mads Moen[6] had the ingenuity
To pop the question while you were flying high
Across the mountains on your deer!

PEER GYNT:

What? He's a Milquetoast! He's a scarecrow!

AASE:

Well, now he's her inamorato.

PEER GYNT:

I'll hitch the horse up—you wait here.

(Starts to go)

AASE:

>Forget the horse and wagon. It's too late.
>Tomorrow they will hold the ceremony.

PEER GYNT:

>I'll arrive long before they consummate
>The marriage.

AASE:

>   Shame on you, Peer! Matrimony
>Isn't a joke! Don't bring me more disgrace—

PEER GYNT:

>You're right, we shouldn't take the wagon—
>It takes too long!

>*(Laughing and shouting simultaneously)*

>   It's all falling into place!
>We're on our way—come on, old dragon!

>*(Lifts her up)*

AASE:

>Let go!

PEER GYNT:

>   I won't. You'll go directly
>To the wedding like a lady—on my arm!

>*(Wades into the river)*

AASE:

>Help! Help! Merciful God protect me!
>We'll drown, Peer!

PEER GYNT:

>   Mother, no cause for alarm,
>For I was born to die a finer death!

AASE:

>Yes, that's for certain! You'll take your last breath
>While hanging in a noose.

(Pulls his hair)

You brute!

PEER GYNT:

Keep quiet, now! It's slippery here.

AASE:

Ass!

PEER GYNT:

Words will never hurt me, dear,
So you just go ahead and shoot
Your mouth off. Almost there, now! See that stump?

AASE:

Peer, don't let go!

PEER GYNT:

Giddyup for the jump!
We're going to play the buck and Peer!

(Gallops)

You will be Peer, and I'm the buck!

AASE:

What can I do—he's run amok!

PEER GYNT *(Walks ashore)*:

We've reached the bank, now pay your fare;
Give your courageous buck a thankful kiss
And say you're sorry for your cowardice.

AASE:

This is my thanks to you, dolt!

(Smacks him on the ear)

PEER GYNT:

Ow!
That's not enough! I feel somehow
I've been shortchanged.

AASE:

Let go!

PEER GYNT:

We'll go at once
To the reception. Make me understood,
Mother; you speak for me. Tell the old dunce
Mads Moen is a clod, that he's no good—

AASE:

Let go of me!

PEER GYNT:

And finally tell
How choice Peer Gynt is. Weave your spell.

AASE:

Oh, Peer, you can bet everything you own—he
Couldn't receive more fitting testimony.
I'll sketch you fore and aft and inside out.
As an example, I'll tell him about
Your damned buffoonery in detail—

PEER GYNT:

Oh?

AASE (Kicks in anger):

And I won't shut up until the old
Man sics his dog on you! I'll scold and scold
Until he hauls you off to jail!

PEER GYNT:

Well, then, I'd better go alone.

AASE:

Go ahead. I'll be right behind you!

PEER GYNT:

Mother, dear, don't do this. Be kind! You—

AASE:

Be kind, eh? I'm so good and mad
That I would gladly eat a stone!

I could break flint! Bend horseshoes! Egad,
I'm mad! Let go!

PEER GYNT:

If you will give your word—

AASE:

Phooey! I'm going to make sure they've heard
About you and know who you are!

PEER GYNT:

No, I can't let you go that far.

AASE:

Too bad! I want to join the celebration!

PEER GYNT:

You can't.

AASE:

How will you stop me?

PEER GYNT *(Puts her on the roof of the mill)*:

You'll stay there
Until we've had a reconciliation.

AASE *(Screams)*:

You get me down right now!

PEER GYNT:

If you will swear—

AASE:

Phooey!

PEER GYNT:

Sweet mother dear, can I allow—

AASE *(Throws grass at him)*:

Peer, you had better get me down right now!

PEER GYNT:

Oh, mother, if I could I would.

(Comes closer)

Don't move around too much. Be good!

Don't kick! You thrash your legs around
Like that, you'll fall flat on the ground!
And if you do don't say I should
Have warned you. Mother dear, goodbye!

AASE:

You swine!

PEER GYNT:

Don't kick!

AASE:

I didn't bear you! You're not mine!
You must have been a changeling!

PEER GYNT:

Mother,

Shame on you!

AASE:

Phooey!

PEER GYNT:

Come on, have you no
Kind word with which to speed me other
Than phooey? Well?

AASE:

You're not too big,
Young man, for me to spank you—so beware!

PEER GYNT:

Mother, goodbye! Be patient, don't despair;
I will return in just a jig.

(Starts to leave, but turns around and lifts a reprimanding finger)

Remember, now, don't kick! So cheerio!

(Leaves)

AASE:

God help me! Peer! Don't leave me on
This roof! Why don't you ride your buck, you boozy

Liar! He's crossed the field—he's gone!

(Screaming)

Help! Anyone! Oh, no! I'm feeling woozy!

(Two old crones with sacks on their backs approach the mill)

FIRST CRONE:

My goodness, who is screaming?

AASE:

Me!

SECOND CRONE:

Aase![7] Well, haven't you come out on top!

AASE:

This situation's bad enough—so stop!

I'd like to just drop dead! I swear!

FIRST CRONE:

Rest in peace!

AASE:

Get a ladder! He

Won't get away with this! Damn you, Peer!

SECOND CRONE:

Your son?

AASE:

That's right, my son! You see

The way he treats me? Is this fair?

FIRST CRONE:

We see.

AASE:

Help me get down from here.

I need to go to Haegstad right away—

SECOND CRONE:

Is that where he went?

FIRST CRONE:

Oh, my dear,

The blacksmith's there! And he still wants to pay
Peer back for Lunde! That fight—
AASE *(Wringing her hands)*:

But they'll kill
My boy! If you don't help him, God, I will!
FIRST CRONE:

They often talk of killing him, that's true!
It's nice that others think about him, too!
SECOND CRONE:

She is demented—she has lost her mind.

(Calls uphill)

Anders! We need some help here—be so kind!
MAN'S VOICE:

Is something wrong?
SECOND CRONE:

You'll never guess where Peer
Has left his mother! On the roof, that's where!

A low hill covered with bushes and heather. A country road can be seen in the background, on the other side of a fence. Peer Gynt comes down a footpath and walks quickly to the fence, stops and looks out at the view.

PEER GYNT:

There's Haegstad's farm! It won't be long.

(Climbs halfway over; then he reconsiders)

If only
Ingrid were waiting there, forlorn and lonely—

(Shades his eyes and looks out)

No, wedding guests are swarming round like flies.
Well, maybe I should just go home.

(Pulls his leg back)

I know
They'll talk behind my back and paralyze
Me with their smirks and sneers and whispers.

*(Walks a few steps away from the fence and pulls at some leaves
distractedly)*

Oh,
If I could only get a good, strong drink!
Or if they didn't know me! If I were
Invisible! But drink is best, I think;
Then I'd be strong—whatever might occur.

*(Starts, looks around, then hides himself behind some bushes. Some
people pass by carrying food, heading downhill to the wedding)*

A MAN *(In conversation)*:
His father was a drunk; his mother—God!
She's sick up here!
A WOMAN:
No wonder he's a clod!

*(The people continue on. Peer Gynt comes forward; his face is beet
red with shame, and he stares after them)*

PEER GYNT *(Softly)*:
Speaking of me?

(Forcing a shrug)

Oh, don't be silly!
Besides, who cares. Their talk can't kill me.

(Throws himself down in the heather and stays there for a long time, lying on his back, hands beneath his head, staring into the sky)

What a strange cloud that is—just like a horse.
I see the reins—a rider in the saddle—
And then behind comes some old crone—astraddle
A broom.

(Laughs quietly)

                That's mother—hollering, of course—
"You swine!" Giddyup, Peer!

(Gradually, his eyes close)

                Leave her behind!
Peer rides ahead as thousands cheer the virtues
Of their Emperor Gynt! Look—golden horseshoes!
Gauntlets, a sword and scabbard—his robe lined
In silk that billows down, down to the ground.
Elegant riders canter all around,
But no one sits his mount as well as Peer
Or shimmers in the sun just so. Look there!—
The crowd's reaction when he passes by—
Men doff their hats and gaze into the sky,
And women curtsy in submission to
Emperor Gynt and his royal retinue.
Shiny gold pieces and coins he throws from side
To side like pebbles. Villagers reside
In princely comfort thanks to his largess.
When Peer travels abroad—they say, *noblesse*
Oblige—the King of England's waiting on the shore
With England's ladies—hundreds—thousands!—maybe
                more!!

And England's king—as soon as Peer appears—
Leads his best people in huzzahs and cheers,
He lifts his crown to Peer and says, "Old chap—"

ASLAK *(Passing by on the other side of the fence)*:

Peer Gynt—look! What a drunken pig!

PEER GYNT *(Startled)*:

Emperor—what!

ASLAK *(Leaning against the fence, chuckling)*:

Get up, bigwig!

PEER GYNT:

Oh, what the hell do you want now, Aslak?

ASLAK *(To the others)*:

The Lunde spirit—ready to attack!

PEER GYNT *(Jumps up)*:

Leave me alone!

ASLAK:

Of course I will, but tell
Us where you've been the last six weeks—Oh, dear,
We worried! Kidnapped by the mountains? Well?

PEER GYNT:

I've done strange things, Aslak!

ASLAK *(Winks at the others)*:

Let's hear!

PEER GYNT:

Forget it.

ASLAK *(After a second)*:

Coming to the wedding, clown?
You might as well since you're so near.

PEER GYNT:

No.

ASLAK:

Wasn't she at one time sweet
On you?

PEER GYNT:
> Bastard!

ASLAK *(Stepping back a little)*:
> Peer, don't retreat!
> So what if Ingrid's turned you down—
> Remember, you're the son of old Jon Gynt!

PEER GYNT:
> Go to hell!

ASLAK:
> Not a one but has a glint
> In her eye for you, Peer—be she Miss or Mrs!
> I'll tell the bride that you send your good wishes!

*(They leave, laughing and whispering. Peer Gynt looks after them
contemptuously and turns around)*

PEER GYNT:
> As far as I'm concerned, that Haegstad wench
> Can marry who she wants—you think I care?

(Looks down)

> My pants are torn and dirty—what a stench!
> If only I had something new to wear.

(Stamps his foot)

> Oh, God, how I would love to knock the scorn
> Right out of them—just one good healthy punch
> Is all that it would take to make that bunch—

(Looks around, jittery)

> What's that? Who's laughing? No one—could have sworn—
> I want my mother.

(He starts uphill, but stops when he hears music down below)

> They've begun to dance.

(Looks and listens, walking downhill one step at a time; his eyes are shining—he rubs his legs)

Oh, what a swarm of girls! This is my chance!
Seven or eight per man! I have to go!
Although I should get mother down, I know . . .

(His gaze is pulled downhill again; he jumps and laughs)

Look at them! Everyone will dance tonight!
Listen to Guttorm play! That's a mean fiddle!
Like a waterfall that sparkles in the light!
Those bubbling girls—I could be in the middle—
But then there's mother—Damn, I have to go!

(Jumps the fence and goes down the road)

The farmyard at Haegstad.[8] The parlor cottage in back. Many guests. Lively dancing in the backyard. The fiddler is sitting on a table. The Master of Ceremonies stands in the door. Several women walk back and forth, carrying food between the buildings; the older people are scattered around, sitting and conversing.

A WOMAN *(Joining a group who are sitting on some logs)*:
    The bride? Oh, yes, she's teary-eyed;
    Ignore it—she's put on her bridal frown.
MASTER OF CEREMONIES *(In another group)*:
    Empty the keg, good people—drink it down!
A MAN:
    No thanks, I'm getting bleary-eyed.
A BOY *(To the fiddler as he flies by with a girl in hand)*:
    Come on, Guttorm, don't spare the strings!

THE GIRL:

Play louder! Till the mountain sings!

GIRLS *(In a circle around a dancing boy)*:

Eeek! What a kick!

FIRST GIRL:

His legs have springs!

BOY *(Dancing)*:

Give me more room, girls! Far and wide!

GROOM *(Sniffling, he approaches his father who's conversing with a couple of other people, and pulls at his jacket)*:

She doesn't want to, father; she's so snooty!

FATHER:

She doesn't want to what?

GROOM:

Open the pantry—

She's locked herself up!

FATHER:

Find the key—Do your duty!

GROOM:

I don't know how—

FATHER:

A man can do it, can't he!

(Returns to his conversation. The groom walks slowly across the yard)

BOY *(From behind the house)*:

Hey, girls, look! Now we're going to have some fun!

Peer Gynt has come.

ASLAK *(Who has just appeared)*:

Huh! Who asked him?

MASTER OF CEREMONIES:

No one.

(Walks toward the house)

ASLAK *(To the girls)*:

    If he says something to you, ignore him!

FIRST GIRL *(To the others)*:

    We'll talk to every other boy before him.

PEER GYNT *(Comes in, warm and lively, stops in front of the girls and claps his hands)*:

    I want the liveliest girl! Who will it be?

FIRST GIRL *(Whom Peer approaches)*:

    Not me!

SECOND GIRL *(As Peer does the same)*:

          Not me!

THIRD GIRL:

               And certainly not me!

PEER GYNT *(Going to a fourth one)*:

    Well, in that case, you'll do until I see

    Anything better.

FOURTH GIRL *(Turning away)*:

          Can't!

PEER GYNT *(To a fifth)*:

          How about you?

FIFTH GIRL *(As she leaves)*:

    I'm going home!

PEER GYNT:

          Tonight? You must be mad!

ASLAK *(In back of him, an audible whisper)*:

    Look at her dance! With that old coot! Too bad!

PEER GYNT *(Turning quickly to an older man)*:

    So where are all the girls?

THE MAN:

          Haven't a clue.

(The man leaves. Peer Gynt suddenly becomes subdued. He glances covertly and shyly at the others. Everyone is looking at him, but no

*one speaks. He walks around to different groups. Whenever he
approaches, they fall silent; when he goes away, they giggle and
stare at him)*

PEER GYNT *(In a low voice)*:
Glances and smirks—they're sharp, they prick—
They cut my heart like a saw cuts a stick.

*(He slinks along the fence. Solveig, with little Helga holding her
hand, comes into the yard with her parents)*

FIRST MAN *(To a second man standing near Peer Gynt)*:
Those are the newcomers.

SECOND MAN:
They're from the West?

FIRST MAN:
That's right—Hedalen.[9]

SECOND MAN:
Yes, I could have guessed.

PEER GYNT *(Steps in front of the newcomers, points to Solveig, and
asks)*:
May I dance with your daughter?

THE MAN *(Quietly)*:
Yes, but first we
Must say hello to those inside.

(They go in)

MASTER OF CEREMONIES *(To Peer Gynt, offering him a drink)*:
Here's mud in your eye! Let's toast the bride!

PEER GYNT *(Gazing after the newcomers)*:
No thank you, I'll be dancing. I'm not thirsty.

*(The Master of Ceremonies leaves. Peer Gynt looks at the house
and laughs)*

I've never seen a girl like that—she glowed!

Her shining eyes cast down to her waistband—
And did you see the way that she tiptoed
Beside her mother, prayer book in hand!
I want another look!

(Starts to go inside)

A BOY *(Coming outside with several others)*:
                    Hey, Peer!

Stopped dancing?

PEER GYNT:
                    No.

A BOY:
                    No girls in there!

(Grabs his shoulders and turns him around)

PEER GYNT:
    Let go!

BOY:
                    Afraid of what the smith will do?

PEER GYNT:
    Afraid?

BOY:
                    Forgotten Lunde, haven't you!

(They head for the dancers, laughing)

SOLVEIG *(In the doorway)*:
    Are you the boy who asked to dance?

PEER GYNT:
    I am. You can't tell at a glance?

(Takes her hand)

    Come on!

SOLVEIG:
                    Not far, you heard my mother say!

PEER GYNT:

Heard mother say? Were you born yesterday?

SOLVEIG:

Don't tease!

PEER GYNT:

Are you a grown-up or a baby?

SOLVEIG:

I was confirmed this Spring.

PEER GYNT:

So grown-up maybe!

Tell me your name—it's easier to talk.

SOLVEIG:

My name is Solveig—what is yours?

PEER GYNT:

Peer Gynt.

SOLVEIG *(Pulling her hand away)*:

Oh, no! My God!

PEER GYNT:

It's such a shock?

SOLVEIG:

My garter's loose—I have to go indoors.

(Leaves)

GROOM *(Tugging at his mother)*:

Mother, she doesn't want to—!

MOTHER:

Want to what?

GROOM:

She doesn't want to, mother!

MOTHER:

What?

GROOM:

Give me the key.

FATHER *(In a low and angry voice)*:
Oh, God! You should be taken out and shot!

MOTHER:
Don't yell at him! Poor thing—my little chickadee!

(They walk on)

BOY *(In a group coming from the dance area)*:
A little moonshine,[10] Peer?

PEER GYNT:
No.

BOY:
Just a little?

PEER GYNT *(Gives him a withering look)*:
Do you have some?

BOY:
Oh, well—I may, I may.

(Pulls out a pocket flask and drinks)

Oh, wow! That burns! And you?

PEER GYNT:
All right, make way!

(Drinks)

SECOND BOY:
Now mine! Well, how about it? Come on, it'll
Do you good.

PEER GYNT:
No!

SECOND BOY:
Oh, come on, milksop;
Drink up!

PEER GYNT:
Well, maybe just a drop.

(Drinks again)

GIRL *(Sotto voce)*:
> Come on, let's go.

PEER GYNT:
> > > > Scared of me, honey?

THIRD BOY:
> Who isn't scared of you?

FOURTH BOY:
> > > > After all, you showed
> Your stuff at Lunde.

PEER GYNT:
> > > That little episode
> Was nothing compared to—what's so funny?

FIRST BOY *(Whispering)*:
> He's warming up!

OTHERS *(Making a circle around him)*:
> > > You were about to say?
> Tell us!

PEER GYNT:
> > > Tomorrow!

OTHERS:
> > > Tell us now, today!

A GIRL:
> Can you do magic?

PEER GYNT:
> > > I can summon Satan!

A MAN:
> Oh, anyone can do that! What a dunce!

PEER GYNT:
> No one can do what *I* can—let me straighten
> You out! I caught him in an acorn once—
> One full of worms, you see!

OTHERS *(Laughing)*:
> > > Easy to see!

PEER GYNT:

> He swore at me and cried and offered me
> This and that—

ONE MAN:

> > Why didn't he come out a hole?

PEER GYNT:

> I plugged them up! You should have heard him roll
> Around inside that shell and growl at me!

A GIRL:

> Just think!

PEER GYNT:

> > He sounded like a bumblebee.

A GIRL:

> Do you still have him in the shell?

PEER GYNT:

> > Oh, no,
> The little charmer took off long ago.
> It's *his* fault that the smith now flinches from me.

A BOY:

> How's that?

PEER GYNT:

> > I asked the smith—polite and chummy—
> If he would help me crack the acorn shell.
> He looked at it, and said, "That's easy, hell!"
> And put it on his anvil. Aslak's strong—
> And you know how he loves to use his hammer—

A VOICE IN THE GROUP:

> He killed the devil?

PEER GYNT:

> > Oh, he banged that shell!
> The Fiend burst out—making a hell of a clamor—
> Shot up in flames and took the roof along.

OTHERS:

And the smith?

PEER GYNT:

He stood there with burnt finger ends,
And since that day we never have been friends.

(Laughter all around)

SOME:

That's not too bad a tale!

OTHERS:

One of his best!

PEER GYNT:

You think I made it up?

MAN:

No, we
Can't say you made it up—you just digest
The tales we've heard—

PEER GYNT:

It happened to me!

MAN:

Everything happened to you!

PEER GYNT *(Combatively)*:

Hey, I can ride
My magic horse across the sky! Suggest
One thing I can't do!—Couldn't if you tried!

(Loud laughter again)

ONE OF THE GROUP:

Go take a ride across the sky, Peer!

OTHERS:

Shoo!

PEER GYNT:

That's just what I will do—so don't entreat.
I'll ride like thunder over all of you

And this whole country will be at my feet!

AN OLDER MAN:

Dumb as a cow!

SECOND ONE:

An idiot, isn't he?

THIRD ONE:

God, what a blowhard!

FOURTH ONE:

Liar!

PEER GYNT *(Threatening all of them)*:

Wait and see!

A MAN *(Half drunk)*:

That's right, wait! You'll get your comeuppance!

SEVERAL:

A black eye! I'll floor him! What impert'nence!

(The group disperses; the older people are angry, the younger ones are teasing and laughing)

GROOM *(Close to Peer)*:

Hey, Peer! They say you ride across the sky!

PEER GYNT *(Curt)*:

That's right, Mads! There is nothing I can't do!

GROOM:

Could you become invisible? Could you?

PEER GYNT:

Invisible? Let's say I won't deny
I can.

(Turns away from him. Solveig crosses the yard holding Helga's hand. Peer Gynt goes toward them, his face lit up)

Solveig! At last you're here!

(Grabs her by the wrists)

I'll dance you to a frenzy, child!

SOLVEIG:

    Let go of me!

PEER GYNT:

              Why?

SOLVEIG:

                    You're too wild!

PEER GYNT:

    The buck gets wild when summer's near.

    Come on, girl! Don't be so quick to condemn!

SOLVEIG *(Pulling away)*:

    Just can't.

PEER GYNT:

           Why not?

SOLVEIG:

                  Because you drink.

(Walks away with Helga)

PEER GYNT:

    Solveig! If only I could sink

    My knife into their hearts—each one of them!

GROOM *(Nudging him with his elbow)*:

    Hey, listen! Help me get the bride.

PEER GYNT *(Absently)*:

    The bride? Where's she?

GROOM:

              She's in the pantry.

    Will you?

PEER GYNT:

        Well—

GROOM:

             We can do it, can't we?

PEER GYNT:

    You do it. I'm preoccupied.

(A thought stops him in his tracks; he speaks quietly and pointedly)

Ingrid! The pantry!

(Approaches Solveig)

Thought it over?

(Solveig tries to leave; he blocks her way)

Embarrassed, girl?—that I look like a tramp?

SOLVEIG *(Quickly)*:

You do not—that's not true!

PEER GYNT:

So what? You'd cramp
My style anyway. Wait! I'm not a scamp,
I'm not some drunken Casanova.
Please dance.

SOLVEIG:

Can't—even if I wanted.

PEER GYNT:

What are you scared of?

SOLVEIG:

Father, mostly.

PEER GYNT:

The quiet one—who has the grim and stunted
Manner? Who looks at you with ghostly
Sanctity?

SOLVEIG:

Please don't!

PEER GYNT:

Isn't he a goody-good?
Are you and mother goody-goods as well?
Are you?

SOLVEIG:

Leave me alone!

PEER GYNT:

No!

(In a terrifying voice, low and harsh)

But I'll tell
You what I'm going to do—I'll join the trolls,
And sneak into your bed when midnight tolls
Tonight! If you hear groaning, in all likelihood
It's me! Don't tell yourself that it's the cat—
It's me! I'll drain your blood into a cup,
Then get your sister! Yes, I'll eat her up!
I'll turn into a werewolf, or a bat,
And bite you on your arms, your neck, your back—

(Abruptly changes mood and timidly begs)

Dance with me, Solveig!

SOLVEIG *(Scowling)*:

You're a maniac!

(Goes in the house)

GROOM *(Meandering out)*:
Give you a pig if you will help!

PEER GYNT:

Why not?

*(They go behind the house. At the same time, a large group is
striding in from the dance area; most of them are drunk. Noise and
excitement. Solveig, Helga, and her parents are coming out of the
door in a group of older people)*

MASTER OF CEREMONIES *(To the smith, who is at the head of the
group)*:
Hold on!

SMITH *(Pulling his shirt off)*:
No! We had settled this, I thought,

Once and for all at Lunde. Now it's him or me—
One of us has to go!

FIRST MAN:

Let 'em fight!

SECOND MAN:

Yes, verbally!

SMITH:

You have to beat it into him; words are no use!

HELGA:

They're going to hit him, mother!

SOLVEIG'S FATHER:

Stop, that's no excuse!

FIRST BOY:

Why not just heckle him about the lie
He told.

SECOND BOY:

Let's kick him out!

THIRD BOY:

Spit in his eye!

FOURTH BOY *(To the Smith)*:

What will you do?

SMITH *(Throwing his shirt down)*:

That pig is tagged for slaughter.

SOLVEIG'S MOTHER *(To Solveig)*:

You see how they respect him, don't you, daughter?

AASE *(Arrives, stick in hand)*:

I'll beat the stuffing out of him! Where is he?
Oh, I will whack him. Oh, I'll bash and bang him!

SMITH *(Rolling up the sleeves of his undershirt)*:

That stick's too soft. I'll beat him till he's dizzy!

FIRST MAN:

The blacksmith wants to get him!

SECOND MAN:

Whip him!

SMITH *(Spits in his hands and nods to Aase)*:

Hang him!

AASE:

Oh, yeah? Go on and do it if you dare!
Aase has teeth and claws, you know! Hang Peer?
My little Peer? Where is he?

(Calls around the farmyard)

Peer!

GROOM *(Running in)*:

Oh, God!

Father—

FATHER:

What's wrong?

GROOM:

Peer Gynt! You never will

Believe it—

AASE *(Screaming)*:

Did they kill him? Say it, clod!

GROOM:

Mother, Peer Gynt—! Peer Gynt—! Up on the hill!

CROWD:

The bride!

AASE *(Dropping her stick)*:

The brute!

SMITH *(In total shock)*:

My God, how he can climb!

He's like a goat!

GROOM *(Crying)*:

He's carrying her away
As if she were a pig, mother!

AASE *(Making threatening gestures)*:
>   I pray
> You fall and break your—!

(Screams in terror)

>   But for the time
> Being, take care!

INGRID´S FATHER *(Coming out bareheaded and white with rage)*:
>   This is abduction! Rape!

> I'll kill him!

AASE:
>   No! Please, God, help him escape!

Act Two

A narrow path, high in the mountains. It's early morning. Peer Gynt walks quickly and stubbornly along the path. Ingrid, her bridal gown partially torn away, tries to hold him back.

PEER GYNT:
Go! Go away!

INGRID *(Crying)*:
Where? After this!

PEER GYNT:
I don't care! Anywhere you say!

INGRID *(Wringing her hands)*:
You lied!

PEER GYNT:
No more unpleasantness!
Each of us goes his separate way.

INGRID:
We can't! Your crimes and mine are ties that bind us!

PEER GYNT:
No! Memory is hell—the devil reminds us!

And devils are women who tag along behind us,
Except for *one*.

INGRID:

And who is that?

PEER GYNT:

Not you.

INGRID:

All right, but tell me who!

PEER GYNT:

Go back to where you came from, you!
Go!

INGRID:

Pretty please! It's just a spat—

PEER GYNT:

Goodbye!

INGRID:

You don't mean that! It's too,
Too cruel.

PEER GYNT:

Yes, I do.

INGRID:

You lead
Me on, then push me off! But why?

PEER GYNT:

What can you give me? Come, reply!

INGRID:

The Haegstad farm! That's guaranteed!

PEER GYNT:

Do you carry a prayer book in your hand?
Do you glow when we are near each other?
Or are your eyes cast down to your waistband?
Do you tiptoe beside your mother?
Answer!

INGRID:
No, but—!
PEER GYNT:
No, but were you confirmed
This spring?
INGRID:
No, but—
PEER GYNT:
Do your eyes shine
With modesty? Are you able to deny me?
INGRID:
He's lost his wits—it's clear! Oh, fine!
PEER GYNT:
Is it a holiday if you pass by me?
Answer!
INGRID:
No, but—!
PEER GYNT:
My judgment's reaffirmed.

(Starts to leave)

INGRID *(Blocking his way)*:
You know, if you walk out on me,
They'll come and get you, and they'll hang you!
PEER GYNT:
Maybe.
INGRID:
But you can have a farm, a wife, a baby—
PEER GYNT:
But at a price I cannot meet!
INGRID *(Breaks into tears)*:
You led me on!

PEER GYNT:

You knew what you were doing!

INGRID:

I was in love!

PEER GYNT:

I was in heat!

INGRID *(Threatening)*:

You'll pay plenty for your deceit!

PEER GYNT:

I'll pay it gladly if it stops your wooing!

INGRID:

You won't change your mind?

PEER GYNT:

It can't be done.

INGRID:

All right! We'll see what happens when they find us!

(Walks down the hill)

PEER GYNT *(Quiet for a while; suddenly, he screams)*:

No! Memory is hell—the devil reminds us!
And devils are women who tag along behind us!

INGRID *(Turns back and calls out sarcastically)*:

Except for *one*!

PEER GYNT:

Except for *one*!

(They go in separate directions)

———————

Beside a mountain lake; the ground is soft and swampy. A storm is brewing. Aase is in despair, shouting and searching in all directions. Solveig has difficulty keeping up with her. The newcomers and Helga are somewhat behind.

AASE *(Waving her arms and tearing her hair)*:
The elements have turned on us—I'm sure to lose him!
These ugly peaks and lakes—even the sky!
Look how the sky is moving fog in to confuse him!
The lakes would like to drown him! The mountains try
To bury him beneath their slides and rubble!
And then these people! Look! They're out to kill
My boy! But I won't let them—damned if I will!

(Turns to Solveig)

The devil is the one who made this trouble!
It's just unthinkable—a thing like this!
So he made up a bunch of fibs! And so
He talked a lot! And never failed to miss
A day of work! So what? I don't know
Whether to laugh or cry! My Peer and I—
We stayed together through both thick and thin.
My husband was a drunk, you see, who'd fly
Around the county with a drunken grin—
Gossiping, throwing all our cash away—
And little Peer and I stayed home, pretending
We didn't notice anything. Each day
I'd lie and say there'll be a happy ending.
For it's not always clear—the writing on the wall;
And people, you know, disregard their sorrow,
Hoping it will be better by tomorrow.
So some resort to lies—and others, alcohol.

Peer and I told each other fairy tales
Of princes, trolls and beasts—living and dead—
Of rape and abduction. Who would think details
Of those damn myths would stick in his thick head?

(Terrified again)

Peer! Way up there! Beyond the riverbed!

*(Runs to a higher spot and looks out over the water. The new-
comers catch up)*

No sign.

MAN *(Quietly)*:

        The worse for him.

AASE *(Crying)*:

          Oh, God, my heart!

Poor little Peer! My poor lost lamb!

MAN *(Nods sympathetically)*:

Yes, he's lost!

AASE:

          That's a lot of damn

Nonsense! There's no one like him! He's so smart—

MAN:

You've been a bad mother!

AASE:

         Yes, understood!

I may be bad—it's true—but Peer is good!

MAN *(Always with a subdued voice and a benign look)*:

No, he is lost. His soul is hardened.

AASE *(Terrified)*:

God's not so rigid! He'll be pardoned!

MAN:

When he has sinned, has he once heaved a sigh?

AASE *(With enthusiasm)*:

No, but he rode a buck across the sky!

WIFE:

Are you insane?

MAN:

What are you saying, mother?

AASE:

He can do anything. One day he'll show
You—if they let him live to see another
Day, that is.

MAN:

I will see him hanged.

AASE *(Screams)*:

Christ, no!

MAN:

For in the hangman's hands, those who
Are unrepentant often turn about.

AASE *(Confused)*:

Please! Stop! Your talk just makes me dizzy! Something tells
Me he's close!

MAN:

Bless his soul!

AASE:

And body, too!

He may be in this swamp; let's pull him out!
If he's been kidnapped by the mountains, ring the bells!

MAN:

Hmm! Here's a cattle path—

AASE:

God, bless you, sir,

For helping!

MAN:

It's our Christian duty.

AASE:

>   Phooey! They're pagans, then! They won't bestir
>   Themselves to help me look for him, the snooty—!

MAN:

>   They know him too well.

AASE:

>   They just envy him!

(Wrings her hands)

>   Because of that his life's at stake!

MAN:

>   A footprint!

AASE:

>   It's a trail—it could be him!

MAN:

>   We should split up now—let's all take
>   More care.

(He and his wife walk on ahead)

SOLVEIG *(To Aase)*:

>   Tell me more!

AASE *(Drying her eyes)*:

>   What? About my son?

SOLVEIG:

>   Everything!

AASE *(Smiles and shakes her head)*:

>   You'd get tired! Yes? Everything?

SOLVEIG:

>   You may well wish that you were done
>   With talking before I'm done with listening.

———————

Low treeless hills in front of a mountain range; peaks farther back.
There are long shadows; it's late in the day.

PEER GYNT *(Enters on the run and stops on the hillside)*:
　　Everyone's beating the bushes for me!
　　They've armed themselves with guns and sticks.
　　　　　　　　　Out front
　　Is old man Haegstad, yelping, leading the hunt,
　　Sounding the warning—Peer is free!
　　Fighting the smith? Phooey! It can't compare!
　　This is real life! You have to be a bear—
　　An animal!

(He jumps around, making fighting gestures)

　　　　　　　And fight against the stream!
　　Pull up the old trees by their roots! Yell! Scream!
　　This is real life! With all its lows and highs!
　　To hell with all those wishy-washy lies!
THREE HERD GIRLS *(Running across the hillside, shouting and singing)*:
　　Come, troll pack! Trond! Kaare and Baard[11]—!
　　Come to our arms! Claim your reward!
PEER GYNT:
　　Who are you calling?
GIRLS:
　　　　　　　　　Trolls! Of course! Of course!
FIRST GIRL:
　　Come to us gently, Trond!
SECOND GIRL:
　　　　　　　　　Baard! Come with force!
THIRD GIRL:
　　Our beds need company! So give us some!

FIRST GIRL:

Ooo! Force is gentle!

SECOND GIRL:

Gentleness—force!

THIRD GIRL:

There are no boys, let's find a horse.

PEER GYNT:

Where are the boys?

ALL GIRLS *(Laughing passionately)*:

Ha, ha! They cannot come!

FIRST GIRL:

Mine called me sweetheart. I was his intended.

He got a frumpy widow when it ended.

SECOND GIRL:

Mine was attracted to a gypsy lass.

He's begging in the street now in Alsace.

THIRD GIRL:

And mine dispatched the love child he helped
make.

Now his head is grinning on a stake.

ALL THREE:

Come, troll pack! Trond! Kaare! Baard—!

Come to our arms! Claim your reward!

PEER GYNT *(Jumps in the middle)*:

I have three heads, one for each maid!

THIRD GIRL:

Think you're that good?

PEER GYNT:

You give the grade!

FIRST GIRL:

To bed! To bed!

SECOND GIRL:

There's ale!

PEER GYNT:

Let it run free!

THIRD GIRL:

Tonight our beds will have some company!

SECOND GIRL *(Kisses him)*:

He's like a red hot iron—he burns and hisses!

THIRD GIRL *(The same)*:

Like an infant's eyes in the blackest pond—these kisses!

PEER GYNT *(Dancing amongst them)*:

My soul is dead, my senses hot,

Smiles on my face, tears in my thoughts!

GIRLS *(Thumbing their noses at the mountains, shouting and singing)*:

Hey, troll pack! Trond! Kaare and Baard!

Did you forget to claim your reward?

(They dance across the hilltop, Peer Gynt in the middle)

In the Ronde[12] mountains. Sunset. Snowcapped peaks around.

PEER GYNT *(Appears dizzy and confused)*:

Castle on top of castle—My!

Look at the shiny gates! No, stay!

Please, stay! They're disappearing! Why?

Now they are gone! They've faded away!

The rooster on the vane has lifted

His wings; he's getting ready to take flight.

Fog has closed in the mountains, drifted

Over the valley, and chased away the light.

Those roots and branches in that barren

Crevice—they look like footprints! Who?

A giant—yes, yes! With feet like a heron—
No doubt they soon will vanish, too.
Why are these rainbows dancing 'round
Before my eyes? They're blinding me!
What is that distant ringing sound?
My eyes—they droop so heavily!
My forehead aches! Oh, God, as if a spike—
No! It's a red hot belt that's squeezing tighter!
Who the hell did this thing to me? It's like—
Oh-oh, my head—it's getting lighter, lighter—

(Sinks down)

I'm flying high over the Gjendin
Ridge—! Poetry—a bunch of goddam lies!
Look there! Beyond the highest linden
Grove—Peer and the bride! Oh, sure, Peer!
                    Exercise
Your elbow! Drink a little more!
Those birds and voices that were after me!
And all those girls—each one a whore!
Lies, lies—a bunch of goddam poetry!

(Stares into space for a long time)

Look at those eagles glide away!
Geese flying south! They fly so easily!
Look at me—stuck in mud and clay
Up to my knees! But why can't I be free!

(Jumps up)

And why can't I fly, too! Be bathed in
Needle-sharp winds washing me clean!
And be baptized again and swathed in
Innocence, like the Nazarene!
I want to leave this grim community,

To fly wherever one finds peace of mind.
I want to sail across the salty sea
And meet the Prince of England! Womankind,
Don't wait for me! Your hopes are all in vain.
This time I'm on my own, so reconcile
Yourselves to that! Oh, well, if it's a strain,
Perhaps I could stop by once in a while.
Now what is this? Those eagles and those rooks—
Oh, what the hell do I care! But that rock
Looks like a gable, and it overlooks
A verdant field in which some stock
Are grazing peacefully—there's not a trace
Of trouble or unrest. The main gate's standing
Open—Aha! I recognize the place!—
It's my grandfather's farm! What a fine thing
It was when it was new! No rags
In the windows—fences in repair—
And all lit up—! Those scalawags
Are partying! A huge affair!
As usual, the pastor smashes
His glass to bits, clinking too hard to get attention
To make a toast. The captain crashes
Against the mirror, and in drunk incomprehension
Mutters, "Oh, my, the pity of it all."
It doesn't matter, mother! Quiet!
With bighearted Jon Gynt hosting the ball,
Everyone joins in the fun and riot—
Hip, hip, hooray! Now everyone
Is shouting! Why all the cacophony?
The captain's calling for Jon's son—
The pastor wants to make a toast to me!
Go in and listen, Jon Gynt's son,

To their paeans of praise—and all for you!
Yes, Peer Gynt, great things thou hast done
And greater things thou shallest do!

(Starts off, runs face first into the mountainside, falls flat on his back and lies there motionless)

A hillside with large trees, rustling leaves. Stars twinkle through the leaves; birds sing in the treetops. A woman dressed in green walks across the hillside. Peer Gynt pursues her making amorous gestures.

WOMAN IN GREEN *(Turns and faces him)*:
    It's true?
PEER GYNT *(Cuts his throat with his finger)*:
                    True as my name is Peer.
As true as you are fair and feminine.
Want me? You'll like the way I care
For you. You won't be asked to weave and spin.
I'll give you food until you think you'll burst.
I'll never pull your hair. You won't be cursed—
WOMAN IN GREEN:
    And you won't beat me, either?
PEER GYNT:
                    Is that likely? Really!
Princes don't beat the gentle sex, at least, ideally.
WOMAN IN GREEN:
    Are you a prince?
PEER GYNT:
                    Yes.

WOMAN IN GREEN:

                    I'm the daughter of the King
Of Dovre.

PEER GYNT:

             Are you, really? Look how all this fits.

WOMAN IN GREEN:

Inside the Ronde mountain father's castle sits.

PEER GYNT:

Oh, well! Mother's is larger than that little thing.

WOMAN IN GREEN:

Do you know of my father? He's King Brose.

PEER GYNT:

Do you know of my mother? She's Queen Aase.

WOMAN IN GREEN:

When father's angry, mountains burst.

PEER GYNT:

Oh, yeah? When mother squawks her worst,
They burp.

WOMAN IN GREEN:

            Father can drive unbroken teams.

PEER GYNT:

Mother can ford the most turbulent streams.

WOMAN IN GREEN:

A little ragged, no? The way you're dressed?

PEER GYNT:

Hey, you should see me in my Sunday best!

WOMAN IN GREEN:

My plainest clothes are silken finery.

PEER GYNT:

They look like refuse from a vinery.

WOMAN IN GREEN:

There's one thing you should keep in mind
About our country ways—you'll find

That each of our possessions has a double.
As an example, if they let you travel
Father's estate, you mustn't let it trouble
You that it seems to be debris and gravel.

PEER GYNT:

Oh, yes, I know—that's just the way it is with us!
Gold looks like rubbish, junk! You'll think it's ludicrous!
Or in our windows, you might think you see—instead
Of rich stained glass—some rags or scraps of old bedspread.

WOMAN IN GREEN:

Black will seem white, and ugly, beautiful.

PEER GYNT:

Large will seem small; defiance, dutiful!

WOMAN IN GREEN *(Throws her arms around his neck)*:

We're made for one another—we're a perfect pair!

PEER GYNT:

Just like an arm in a sleeve; just like a comb in the hair.

WOMAN IN GREEN *(Shouting toward the surrounding hills)*:

Come, bridal horse! Here, bridal horse! Come here!

(A huge pig comes running toward them, a piece of cord for a halter, an old sack for a saddle. Peer Gynt swings himself up and pulls the Woman in Green on in front of him)

PEER GYNT:

Let's go! I'm now your Ronde cavalier!
Gee-up! Gee-up, my noble steed! Let's go!

WOMAN IN GREEN *(Affectionately)*:

Just when I was so lonely, so off-course!
All I can say is—boy, you never know!

PEER GYNT *(Whipping the pig and continuing on)*:

You know a man by how he sits his horse!

———————

The royal hall of the Old Man of Dovre. A large congregation of gnomes, goblins and troll people. The Old Man of Dovre on a throne, with his crown and scepter. His children and closest relatives on either side. Peer Gynt stands in front of him. Much commotion in the hall.

TROLLS:

Kill him! Son of a Christian! Kill him! Didn't he
Seduce the Old Man's favorite daughter!

FIRST TROLL CHILD:

May I slice off his finger?

SECOND TROLL CHILD:

Daddy, let
Me bite him! Let me pull his hair!

TROLL GIRL:

Let's get
Him where it hurts!

FIRST TROLL WITCH *(Holding a ladle)*:

Why not just slaughter
The pig and throw him in my soup!

SECOND TROLL WITCH *(Holding a cleaver)*:

But isn't he
A perfect piece for broiling on my spit!

OLD MAN OF DOVRE:

Cool off!

(Beckons his advisors closer)

Let's not be hasty. Think a bit.
The last few years, our backsides have been showing!
We don't know if we're coming or we're going,
So let's not push away a helping hand,
Not even if it's human! He's not grand,
But he's not bad, either, it seems to me.

It's true he only has one head, but look—
My daughter's just the same. No one has three
Heads anymore. The younger ones forsook
The fashion—even two are hard to find,
And they aren't half as good as one, combined.

(To Peer Gynt)

So you would like to have my daughter?
PEER GYNT:
    Your daughter and your kingdom, yes!
OLD MAN OF DOVRE:
                    You may
Have half for now, you little plotter.
You'll have the other when I pass away.
PEER GYNT:
    That's good enough for me.
OLD MAN OF DOVRE:
                  Hold on, my friend!
You also have some promises to give.
Break *one*, and our relationship will end.
Moreover, you won't be allowed to live.
First, you will notice, no one ever mentions
Any event outside of the dimensions
Of Ronde. Stay away from daylight and good deeds—
PEER GYNT:
    To be the king, that's no great imposition.
OLD MAN OF DOVRE *(Rising from his throne)*:
    And now to test your wits a bit.
OLDEST TROLL *(To Peer Gynt)*:
                He who succeeds
The Old Man of Dovre must have erudition
Enough to solve the royal riddle.

OLD MAN OF DOVRE:

                              If you can,
    Tell me the difference between a troll and man.
PEER GYNT:
    There is no difference—not that I can see.
    Big trolls would like to eat you; small ones scare you.
    Say how that's different from us, I dare you.
OLD MAN OF DOVRE:
    True, there's a certain similarity.
    But morning is morning; night is night.
    There's a difference—they're not quite
    The same—and I would be delighted
    To point it out. Under their skies of blue,
    The humans say, "To thine own self be true!"
    But in the darkness of the mountain bluff,
    Trolls say, "To thine own self be true enough!"
OLDEST TROLL *(To Peer Gynt)*:
    You see it, don't you?
PEER GYNT:
                              I'm nearsighted.
OLD MAN OF DOVRE:
    That penetrating word, "Enough," alarms
    You, but it must be in your coat of arms.
PEER GYNT *(Scratching behind his ear)*:
    Well—
OLD MAN OF DOVRE:
              Must—if thou shalt be a king, my lad.
PEER GYNT:
    Really? Oh, hell, why not? It's not so bad.
OLD MAN OF DOVRE:
    And finally you must learn to love and praise
    Our homespun way of life, our simple ways.

(He waves. Two trolls with pigs' heads, white nightcaps, etc., bring in food and drink)

Cows give us pies, oxen give meat;
Don't ask if the drink's sour or sweet—
No matter—eat! Don't be afraid!
The thing that counts is it's homemade.

PEER GYNT *(Pushes it all away)*:
To hell with all your homemade food
And country ways!

OLD MAN OF DOVRE:
                                    Now don't be rude!
The bowl goes with the food—it's gold! Of course
The daughter goeth with the bowl, perforce.

PEER GYNT *(Thinking it over)*:
Well, nature must obey necessity,
They say. I can't be too persnickety.
Why not?

(He gives in)

OLD MAN OF DOVRE:
                                    Now that was done with real finesse.
You spit?

PEER GYNT:
                                    Habit will help the taste, I guess.

OLD MAN OF DOVRE:
You look so Christian—human!—in that clothing.
Throw it out! What you'll wear if you're betrothing
My daughter must be mountain-made—and without fail—
Except, perhaps, the silken bow that tips your tail.

PEER GYNT *(Angry)*:
I have no tail!

OLD MAN OF DOVRE:

               Then thou shallst hav'st one now!
My Sunday tail, please! Tie it on somehow.

PEER GYNT:

You can't! I'll be the laughing stock of all mankind!

OLD MAN OF DOVRE:

Don't ever court my daughter with a bare behind!

PEER GYNT:

You'd make a man a beast?

OLD MAN OF DOVRE:

               It would be truer
To say we're making you a fitting wooer.
Now we'll tie on a yellow ribbon. There!
Our highest honor for a derrière!

PEER GYNT *(Thoughtfully)*:

They say that man is just a speck—it's true!—
And when in Rome you know what you should do.
Well, tie away!

OLD MAN OF DOVRE:

               Thou be-est a pleasant fellow!

OLDEST TROLL:

Move 'round! Feel how it wags and swings!

PEER GYNT *(Annoyed)*:

I won't. Why should I do these things?
Must I also renounce my faith in God?

OLD MAN OF DOVRE:

You're welcome to keep that. We think it's odd
But we won't charge you for it. Faith is free.
Trolls know each other by their scabs, you see,
So if the clothing's similar, and the rear,
You're welcome to your faith—which we call fear.

PEER GYNT:

Despite it all, you are more moderate than

I thought you'd be.

OLD MAN OF DOVRE:

Son, if the implication
Is that we're better than our reputation,
You're right. It's another way that trolls and man
Are not alike. An end to gravity!
Let's have some fun! Let's hear the Dovre harp
Play now, my dear; come out! Dancers, look sharp!
This very moment! We need levity!

(Music and dancing)

OLDEST TROLL:

What's wrong?

PEER GYNT:

Wrong? Oh . . .

OLD MAN OF DOVRE:

What do you think?

Speak up!

PEER GYNT:

They're terrible! They stink!
A cow is banging some contraption with its hoof!
A sow is stumbling 'round the room in stockings!
Oof!

TROLLS:

Eat him!

OLD MAN OF DOVRE:

Now wait—he has human perception!

TROLL GIRLS:

Rip his ears off! We'll tear your eyes out, mister!

WOMAN IN GREEN *(Crying)*:

Boohoo! Must we put up with this? My sister
And I gave him a beautiful reception!

PEER GYNT:

    Oh, was it you? Come on, I'm only teasing!
    It was a joke! You know I didn't mean it!

WOMAN IN GREEN:

    You swear?

PEER GYNT:

                Yes! It was altogether pleasing,
    Cross my heart! I'm so lucky to have seen it!

OLD MAN OF DOVRE:

    This human nature is peculiar, eh?
    Impossible to rid yourself of it!
    When, in a fight with us, it's gashed a bit
    It scars and then is mended right away.
    My son-in-law is most accommodating—
    He chucked his Christian clothes, no hesitating;
    Willingly he drank all our mead,
    And willingly he tied a tail on his behind.
    He was so willing to proceed,
    In truth, with everything we asked, I was inclined
    To think we'd made Old Adam disappear
    Once and for all; then, presto! he's right here
    In front of us again. Son, if we're to do in
    Your human nature, you must take your medicine.

PEER GYNT:

    What are you doing?

OLD MAN OF DOVRE:

              I will scratch one eye
    A little bit—your vision will be skewed,
    But everything you see will be imbued
    With symmetry. The other I'll cut out—

PEER GYNT:

    You're drunk!

OLD MAN OF DOVRE *(Places some sharp instruments on the table)*:
>   My glazier's tools! We will apply
>   Blinders, just like an angry bull—no doubt
>   You'll then detect my daughter's pulchritude.
>   Never again will stumbling sows
>   Offend your sight, or musical cows—

PEER GYNT: ·
>   You're talking like you're crazy!

OLDEST TROLL:
>   Quiet, lad!
>   The Old Man's wise; you're the one who's mad!

OLD MAN OF DOVRE:
>   Just think of how much pain and suffering
>   You will avoid over the days and years.
>   Remember—eyes are the gathering
>   Place for the bitter burning pool of tears.

PEER GYNT:
>   That's true! The Good Book recommends,
>   Of course, that if thine eye offends
>   Thee, slice it out. Listen! How long before they mend
>   And I'm myself again.

OLD MAN OF DOVRE:
>   Never again, my friend.

PEER GYNT:
>   Oh, well, then! Well! In that case, thank you and goodbye!

OLD MAN OF DOVRE:
>   What are you doing?

PEER GYNT:
>   I'm afraid I have to fly.

OLD MAN OF DOVRE:
>   Whoa! Getting in is easy, but the gate
>   Of Dovre doesn't open out.

PEER GYNT:

                              Now wait
    One minute here! You can't force me to stay!
OLD MAN OF DOVRE:

    Listen! Be sensible, Prince Peer, my son!
    You have a gift for trolldom. I might say
    You can't become a troll because you're one
    Already. You would like to join us, right?
PEER GYNT:

    God, yes! To get a wife and an empire?
    And in return, there are things you require,
    I know, but there are limits! It is quite
    True that I willingly tied on a tail,
    But it can be untied! I don't bewail
    The clothing that I cast aside; I'll get
    It back and put it on, and—hell!—I bet
    I look as good as ever, and I can throw
    Your homespun way of life overboard, no
    Trouble at all! I swore cows sang like birds—
    An oath, you say!—well, I can eat my words!
    But to know I can't be a free man—ever!—
    To know I can't be buried properly,
    To know I'll be a mountain troll forever!
    And can't return to that which used to be!
    Well, as they say, *that* makes me stop and think!
    No, no, I can't—no matter how much stink
    You raise.
OLD MAN OF DOVRE:

                    I'm goddam angry, son,
    And when that happens, I'm no fun
    To deal with. Do you know, you popinjay,
    Who I am? First you lead my child astray—

PEER GYNT:

You lie!—

OLD MAN OF DOVRE:

What's that? You weren't her admirer?
You didn't yearn for her? Didn't desire her?

PEER GYNT *(With a snort)*:

Desire! Who gives a damn?

OLD MAN OF DOVRE:

Friends, I suspect
This thing called human nature cannot change.
They talk and talk of peace and love! It's strange
Then that there's only one thing they respect,
And that's brute force! What you desired
Doesn't count, eh? Seeing is believing, Peer!

PEER GYNT:

You won't get me to bite on that one!

WOMAN IN GREEN:

Ere
The year is out, we'll have the child you sired!

PEER GYNT:

Open the door—I'm going!

OLD MAN OF DOVRE:

You can wrap the child
In buckskin!

PEER GYNT *(Mopping up the perspiration)*:

God, I wish this dream would end!

OLD MAN OF DOVRE:

Shall he be sent straight to your castle?

PEER GYNT:

Send
Him to an orphanage!

OLD MAN OF DOVRE:

It will be reconciled

In any case, by you, Prince Peer. What's done
Is done, and one thing's sure—item: your progeny
Will grow and grow. These hybrids bloom like villainy—

PEER GYNT:

Old man, don't be so stubborn! Anyone,
Help! Reason with him, girl! Let's compromise.
You know I'm no fine prince. You recognize
By now no matter how you weigh or measure me,
I'll never add much to your treasury.

(The Woman in Green cries out in pain and is carried out by Troll Girls)

OLD MAN OF DOVRE *(Looks at him for a moment with complete contempt; then he says)*:
Smash him against the mountainside,
Children!

TROLL CHILDREN:
                    A new game! Peericide!
Oh, let's play owl and eagle! Cat and mouse!
The wolf game!

OLD MAN OF DOVRE:
                    Hurry! Rid me of this louse!
Goodnight!

(Leaves)

PEER GYNT *(Being chased by the Troll Children)*:
                    You little devils! Stop! No more!

(Tries to crawl up the chimney)

TROLL CHILDREN:
Gnomes! Goblins! Bite his tail!

PEER GYNT:
                    Ouch!

(Tries to open a trap door to the cellar)

TROLL CHILDREN:

Close the door!

OLDEST TROLL:

What a good time! Look at the little shaver!

PEER GYNT *(Fighting with a Troll Child whose teeth are clamped on his ear)*:

Let go, you tick!

OLDEST TROLL *(Rapping him across the knuckles)*:

You scamp! Watch your behavior!

That child's highborn!

PEER GYNT:

A rat hole!

(Runs toward it)

TROLL CHILDREN:

Block it!

PEER GYNT:

Curse

You all! The Old One's bad, but the young are worse!

TROLL CHILDREN:

Skin him!

PEER GYNT:

If only I were little as a mouse!

(Running to and fro)

TROLL CHILDREN *(Surrounding him)*:

Quick, close him in!

PEER GYNT *(Crying)*:

How do I leave this crazy house!

(He falls down)

TROLL CHILDREN:

Go for his eyes!

PEER GYNT *(Buried in the pile of trolls)*:
                    Help, mother, or I'll die!

(Church bells ring in the distance)

TROLL CHILDREN:
    Achh! Bells! Run, run! There must be priests nearby!

*(The Trolls run away in bedlam, howling and screaming. The hall
collapses; everything disappears)*

*Pitch darkness. Peer Gynt can be heard thrashing and flailing
around with a large branch.*

PEER GYNT:
    Who are you? Speak!
A VOICE IN THE DARKNESS:
                    Myself!

PEER GYNT:
                        Out of my way!
VOICE:
    Go 'round! There's room enough, wouldn't you say?
PEER GYNT *(Tries to get through in another spot, but is blocked)*:
    Who are you?
VOICE:
                    Myself, Peer! Can you say the same?
PEER GYNT:
    Me? I say what I want! This is no game!
    Hoo-ha! Be careful of my sword! They say King Saul
    Crushed hundreds of assailants—Peer Gynt crushes all!

(He thrashes and flails)

Who are you?

VOICE:

Myself.

PEER GYNT:

That asinine reply
Is growing old. It doesn't clarify
Anything. *What* are you?

VOICE:

The Great Between.

PEER GYNT:

Oh, say!
A riddle that was black now is looking gray!
Out of the way, Between!

VOICE:

Peer, go around!

PEER GYNT:

Through!

(He thrashes and flails)

Now he's down!

(Tries to go forward, but is blocked)

They fall, then they rebound!

VOICE:

The Great Between, Peer Gynt! There's only one.
I am Between—triumphant and undone.
I am the Great Between—dead and alive.

PEER GYNT *(Throws the branch down)*:

Trolls may beat down my sword, but fists will drive
Through anything!

(Tries to break through)

VOICE:

Ha! Trust your muscles, Peer!

Yes, trust your fists! You can go anywhere!

PEER GYNT *(Trying again)*:

It's just as far, forward or back;
Outside or in looks just as black!
He's *there*! He's *there*! And now he's there—surrounding
Me just when I think I've escaped! Astounding!
Speak up! Move! Let me see you! Who are you?

VOICE:

Between.

PEER GYNT *(Groping around)*:

Not dead. And not alive. Then who
Can say it's human? Hibernating bears,
Perhaps, are growling at me from their lairs.

(Shouts)

Come out and fight!

VOICE:

Between is not insane.

PEER GYNT:

Fight!

VOICE:

There's no need to fight Between.

PEER GYNT:

My brain
Is going! Fight!

VOICE:

The Great Between, of course,
Prevails without a fight.

PEER GYNT:

If he were just a gnome—
Something that I could touch! If he were less
Elusive, or a troll! I wish that I were home!
Between!

VOICE:

What now?

PEER GYNT:

Stop snoring! Use some force—

VOICE:

The Great Between will win with gentleness.

PEER GYNT *(Biting his arms and hands)*:

Bite through the skin, Peer Gynt! Give it a pinch!
I want to feel your blood come spurting through.

(A sound like the beating of large wings)

A BIRD CALL:

Coming, Between?

VOICE:

He's coming, inch by inch.

BIRD CALL:

Come, sisters, fly! Fly to our rendezvous!

PEER GYNT:

Girl, can you save me? If so, do it quickly!
Stop looking at your waistband, bent and sickly,
Clasping your bible! Throw it in his face—don't miss!

BIRD CALL:

Look, he's deranged.

VOICE:

He's ours.

BIRD CALL:

Fly twice

As fast! Fly, sisters!

PEER GYNT:

For an hour like this
Life comes at much too high a price.

(Collapses)

BIRDS:

He's down, Between! Sisters, go find him! Find him!

(In the distance, bells are ringing and psalms are being sung)

BETWEEN *(Gasping as he vanishes)*:
He's much too strong! Women are behind him.

Sunrise. A mountainside. The door of Aase's little cabin is closed; it is secluded and quiet. Peer Gynt is asleep beside the cabin.

PEER GYNT *(Wakes up, looks around with a dull, heavy expression. He spits)*:
What I'd give for a salty herring!

(Spits again and as he does, he sees Helga, who is approaching him carrying a basket of food)

Hi, kid! What's that you have? You sharing
Your dinner with me?
HELGA:
                    Solveig—
PEER GYNT *(Jumping to his feet)*:
                              Where is *she?*
HELGA:
Behind the cabin.
SOLVEIG *(From hiding)*:
                    Don't come near me or I'll run!
PEER GYNT *(Stops)*:
What are you scared of girl? Afraid we'll have some fun?
SOLVEIG:
Shame on you!

PEER GYNT:

Bet you don't know how I spent last night!
Flirting! That Dovre girl is like a flea—
Can't shake her off.

SOLVEIG:

That's why they rang the bells.

PEER GYNT:

But I'm not one who kisses and then tells—
What did you say?

HELGA *(In tears)*:

She's going—can't you be polite?

(Runs after her)

Wait!

PEER GYNT *(Grabs her arm)*:

Here's a gift—to show my gratitude!
Here, kid, take this—a silver button. Just
For you. But do speak well of me. You must!

HELGA:

Let go! Let go of me!

PEER GYNT:

Here!

HELGA:

There's the food.

PEER GYNT:

God help you if you don't speak—!

HELGA:

You upset me!

PEER GYNT *(Meekly; letting her go)*:

I meant to say, tell her please don't forget me!

(Helga runs away)

Act Three

Deep in a pine forest. Gray autumn weather. Snowfall. Peer Gynt is in his shirt sleeves chopping timber.

PEER GYNT *(Chopping at a large pine tree with crooked branches)*:
Oh, yeah, I know you're tough, old man,
But that won't help; you're going to fall.

(Continues chopping)

My sword, you see, is stronger than
Your armor—it will cut through all
Your steel. Don't wave your crooked arms at me
And tremble so goddam hysterically;
It does no good—you'll soon be on your knees—

(Suddenly stops chopping)

Lies! There is no one here! Nothing but trees!
Lies! Lies! This is no gallant knight
Who's dressed in armor. It's a pine—with a break
In the bark. Wood chopping is no easy chore!
When you try both to chop and fight,
It's hell! These fantasies must stop! No more

Of this! Lost in the clouds, fully awake!

(Chops for a while rapidly)

You are an outlaw, boy! Daydreams won't make
That any different. Mother isn't able
To cook the food for you and set your table,
So help yourself! If you want to eat,
There's fish in the river—in the woods, there's meat!
Chop your own kindling, boy; make your own fire,
Look after yourself! Fix everything
Yourself! Want a warm coat? Then catch
A deer! You want a house? Then bring
The rocks down to the clearing! Oh, you require
Logs—cart them on your back! And the thatch—

(The axe falls down; he gazes ahead)

Oh, it will be so beautiful. Turrets and towers
Above, and in each window, a box of flowers.
I'll carve a mermaid—as a decoration—
On the gable—modest in configuration,
Of course! The vanes and locks of solid brass!
Neighbors, accustomed to the dark
Forest, will wonder at the spark
They see when sunlight hits the window glass!

(An angry laugh)

Damn! That's a lie! You're doing it again.
You are an outlaw, boy!

(Chops vigorously)

        A roof of plain
And simple bark keeps out the wind and rain.

(Looks up at the tree)

He's teetering! A swift kick in the shin
Will send him sprawling. Won't the other trees
Tremble and shake to see him on his knees!

(Starts to chop again; he stops, axe raised above his head, and listens)

Someone is there! I'd better keep an eye out
For old man Haegstad—he's a tricky one!

(Dives behind the tree and peeks out)

A boy! Alone—seems to be on the lookout
For someone. Huh! I wonder what he's done.
What's that? A sickle. Now he looks around
Again, hand on the fence post. He lingers
There for a moment, looking at the ground—
Now what? Oh, no! One of his fingers!
He cut it off! My God, look at the blood!

(Stands up)

He left his finger lying in the mud
And ran away! An irretrievable
Finger—destroyed! It's unbelievable!
Oh, I see—! That way he'll avoid the draft!
He's needed, but he doesn't want to go,
And now they'll have to say that he's unfit!
But cutting off your finger—I don't know—
You cut it off *forever*! No, that's daft!
Yes, thinking it! Or even wanting it!
But *do*ing it? I'm not that desperate!

(Shakes his head, then goes back to work)

Inside Aase's cottage. Everything is in disorder; chests are open; clothing is spread around; a cat on the bed. Aase and the cotter's wife are busy packing and moving things around.

AASE *(Running to one side of the room)*:
Listen here, Kari!
KARI:
                    Now what?
AASE *(Running back)*:
                    Listen here—!
Where is—? Where can I find the—?
                    Tell me where—?
What am I after? It's like I'm in shock!
Where is the key to the box?
KARI:
                    It's in the lock.

AASE:
What is that noise?
KARI:
                    It's the last wagon load
Going to Haegstad.
AASE *(Crying)*:
                    This whole episode
Will kill me—put me in a wooden box!
How much can a poor woman stand? A pox
On all of them! The house is bare.
What old man Haegstad left, the sheriff took as tax.
They didn't want to leave the clothes upon our backs.
They had no pity!—Wasn't their concern!

(Sits on the edge of the bed)

The farmhouse and the land are gone. It's perverse
How tough the old man was, but the court was worse.

Shame on them—they were so unfair!
With Peer away, to whom was I to turn?

KARI:

But you can stay here while you're living.

AASE:

Manna from heaven! They're so giving!

KARI:

He has cost you a pretty penny, mother.

AASE:

Peer? Not at all. You're all mixed up! Another
Thing to remember—Ingrid came home safe
And sound! The devil is the one that they
Should punish, not my boy! My little waif
Was innocent—Satan led him astray!

KARI:

Perhaps it's time for us to ask the pastor
To come. You're not aware how bad things are.

AASE:

The pastor? Yes, perhaps—I'm going faster—

(Gets up quickly)

But I'm his mother—God no! I can't be far
Away when he's in need! My obligation
Is here! I am the person who must never
Fail him—Look here! His sweater—would it ever
Be mended if I weren't here? Damnation!
If only I had kept the furs! And where
Are his pants?

KARI:

                    There, in the trash.

AASE *(Rummaging through the things)*:

                              What's this? Oh, no,
His old casting ladle, Kari—let me show

You this—he would play button-molder there
On the floor, melting and shaping. Once, in the middle
Of a loud party, he asked Jon for a little
Pewter. His father said, "No pewter, lad!
You're Jon Gynt's son! You fill that mold
With silver!" He had been drinking, I might add,
And couldn't tell pewter from gold.
Look at these pants. Holes in the holes. How sad!
I have to mend them, Kari!

KARI:

                              Here's some thread.

AASE:

And when I'm finished, I'll go back to bed.
Oh, my, I feel so weak, so rotten—

(Happily)

Look, two wool shirts—they were forgotten!

KARI:

Yes, so it seems.

AASE:

                    They could be put to use.
Let's take one! Why not both! The cotton
Shirt that he's wearing is a poor excuse
For clothing, Kari—it's so worn and thin!

KARI:

But mother Aase, stealing is a sin!

AASE:

Pastor says if you make a resolution
To steal no more, then God grants absolution.

————————

Outside a newly-built cabin in the woods. Reindeer antlers over the door. The snow is deep. It is getting dark. Peer Gynt is outside the door working on a large wooden bolt with his hammer.

PEER GYNT *(Laughing fitfully)*:
> I'll lock out women, lock out men,
> I'll lock out trolls and demons, then
> I'll make a lock to guard my home
> Against the worst—the Dovre gnome!
> Trolls come in the dark; they clap and shout, "You cannot
> Forget us, Peer Gynt; we're quicker than a thought!
> In the ashes or under the bed we do this and that
> Or flick up the chimney like a burning gnat.
> Hee-hee! Peer Gynt! Those nails cannot
> Keep out a furious demon thought!"

(Solveig arrives, skiing across the moor; she has a scarf on her head and a bundle in her hand)

SOLVEIG:
> God bless your work. Oh, please don't turn away.
> You sent for me; you have to let me stay.

PEER GYNT:
> Solveig! It can't be—! Yes, and you appear
> To be—! You're not afraid of coming here?

SOLVEIG:
> Helga brought me your message. Another day
> There was a message on the wind, and in my sigh.
> Your mother brought a message with every word
> She spoke. In every single dream I heard
> Your message. The endless nights and empty days
> Brought me your message. Now my heart obeys;
> I've come. My life was passing by;
> I couldn't laugh, I couldn't cry.

Whether or not you feel the same thing, too,
I've come. I only know what I must do.

PEER GYNT:

Your father?

SOLVEIG:

In this world, I've no one other
Than you. I have no father. I have no mother.
I've cut myself off; now I'm on my own.

PEER GYNT:

Solveig—to be with me?

SOLVEIG:

Yes. You alone.
A friend needs comfort, Peer! Can you assist her?

(In tears)

I'm sorry. It was hard to leave my sister.
And leaving father—that was even worse!
Walking away, though, from the one who nursed
Me at her breast—oh, that, I think was worst
Of all! Will I, in all this universe,
Obtain forgiveness?

PEER GYNT:

You know what's been done to me?
The judge took my inheritance, my farm—

SOLVEIG:

I've left my home and family! Do you think I've
Done that because I wanted wealth and property?

PEER GYNT:

You know there's nowhere we are safe from harm?
That anyone can take me in—dead or alive.

SOLVEIG:

Today I asked directions at a farmstead;
The farmer said, "Where are you going?" I said,

"I'm going home."

PEER GYNT:

                     Furious demons thought
They could undo me. Nails and boards cannot
Keep them out, but if you are willing to
Remain, this cabin, though it's bare,
Is sacred! Solveig, let me look at you—
Just look! You are so bright! So fair!
Now let me carry you! Oh, yes! How nice and light!
Carrying you, Solveig, I'll never tire.
With outstretched arms I'll hold you, and admire
You from afar—I'll never soil you, my delight,
My lovely one! Who would have thought that you—!
I've longed for you both day and night! And when
I built this house, I thought of you! It's too
Ugly—I'll tear it down and start again!

SOLVEIG:

Ugly or not, it's where I want to be—
Fresh air—easy to breathe! It's not the same
Down there—it's so oppressive. *That*, you see,
Is partly why I left them, why I came
Up here, to hear the rustling of the pine,
The peace and quiet—of a home.

PEER GYNT:

                     You're not mistaken?
For your whole life?

SOLVEIG:

                  I'm sure; the steps that I have taken
Peer, cannot be retraced.

PEER GYNT:

                   Then you are mine!
And every single thing that I require
Is here. Go in! I'll get some wood. A fire

Will make the cottage cozy and bright and warm,
And we shall sit there, heedless of the storm.

(He opens the door; Solveig goes in. He stands still for a moment, then bursts out laughing and jumps up and down with happiness)

My princess! My protectress! My salvation!
At last my castle has a firm foundation!

(He grabs the axe and starts off; at the same moment, an elderly woman in a ragged green dress comes out of the bushes, followed by an ugly brat who limps behind her, holding onto her skirt, and carrying a jug)

WOMAN IN GREEN:
Well, Mr. Now-you-see-him-now-you-don't!
PEER GYNT:
Who—?
WOMAN IN GREEN:
We're old friends, Peer Gynt! My house is near.
We're neighbors.
PEER GYNT:
I was not aware of that.
WOMAN IN GREEN:
My house grew large while you were building here.
PEER GYNT *(Starts to go)*:
I have to go—
WOMAN IN GREEN:
Oh, sure, that's fine; we won't
Be far behind you.
PEER GYNT:
You're mistaken, mother!
WOMAN IN GREEN:
I was mistaken once before—another
Promise you broke—

PEER GYNT:

What are you getting at?
What in the hell is this?
WOMAN IN GREEN:

That misbegotten
Night that you met my father—you've forgotten?
PEER GYNT:

I can't forget something I never knew!
What do you mean? When did I last meet you?
WOMAN IN GREEN:

The last time was the first time.

(To the brat)

Darling, why
Not give your dad a drink—I think he's dry.
PEER GYNT:

Your dad? You're drunk! You're telling me—?
WOMAN IN GREEN:

You know a pig by his skin! This is the same!
Do you have eyes? Can you not see
His leg is lame the way your brain is lame?
PEER GYNT:

You think that I—?
WOMAN IN GREEN:

Don't try to wriggle out—
PEER GYNT:

That vile long-legged brat—!
WOMAN IN GREEN:

They quickly sprout.
PEER GYNT:

Hey, pig face, you aren't going to outfox—
WOMAN IN GREEN:

Oh, you're about as tactful as an ox!

(Cries)

I know today I'm not the striking beauty
I was when you performed your so-called duty!
I've been in labor! I've been bedeviled!
Of course I look a bit disheveled!
But if you'd like me charming as before,
Just show your mademoiselle in there the door.
Drive the tart out of sight and mind, my dear,
And if you do, this snout will disappear!

PEER GYNT:

Away, you witch!

WOMAN IN GREEN:

Not till the day I die!

PEER GYNT:

I'll smack you in the—!

WOMAN IN GREEN:

Go ahead and try!
Oh, I'll take care of you—I'll make you pay,
Peer Gynt! I'll return every single day!
I'll crack the door, and watch you two
Getting all lovey-dovey on the bench,
And when you try to pitch your woo,
Peer Gynt, I'll be between you and the wench
To get my share. We can take turns!
It won't be hard once your dear learns
Her part!

PEER GYNT:

You bitch!

WOMAN IN GREEN:

Oh, I almost forgot!
You get to raise the brat, you footloose sot!
Babykins, go to daddy!

BRAT *(Spits on him)*:

                      Phooey! I'll chop

His head off with the axe! I'll get you, pop,

Just wait!

WOMAN IN GREEN *(Kisses the brat)*:

                    He's such a cute son-of-a-gun!

Just goes to show—right, Peer?—like father, like son!

PEER GYNT *(Stamping his foot)*:

I wish you were as far—

WOMAN IN GREEN:

                    As we are near!

PEER GYNT *(Wringing his hands)*:

And all because of what?

WOMAN IN GREEN:

                  Desire, my dear!

You did me wrong!

PEER GYNT:

                  But someone else is hurt!

Solveig! My purest treasure!

WOMAN IN GREEN:

                It's the devil's way—

The mommy beats the child when daddy goes astray.

The sinner never gets his just dessert!

(She trudges into the forest with the brat, who flings the jug at Peer)

PEER GYNT *(After a long pause)*:

Go 'round, the Great Between says. I have to do that here.

My castle's tumbled down in thunder and in hail!

A wall is now between us, just as she drew near.

Everything's been corrupted! All my joy is stale!

Boy, go around! There's no road through

What stands between that girl and you.

No road through? Maybe I could find a way.
There's something called contrition, so they say;
What is it, though? It's written in what book?
Who cares? I'm in the forest—I can't look
It up! No, that won't get me off the hook.
Contrition? Sure, and wonders never cease!
I won't find that road through. Oh, please—don't whine!
When you break something beautiful and fine,
You can't glue it together piece by piece!
A violin—maybe—but not a bell!
Beautiful flowers don't grow very well
When trampled on! That pig witch and her troglodyte
Are gone—at least that ugliness is out of sight.
Out of my sight—oh, yes—but not my mind.
The dirty thoughts all tag along behind.
Ingrid! Those other three! Will all of them return
And want to come along? Will they insist,
Laughing maliciously, that they should have their turn,
Be carried in my arms, enjoy a tryst?
Boy, go around! My outstretched arms could be
As long as pine boughs; higher than the highest trees
I could be holding her—and still the dirt
Would blacken her, and that dirt comes from me.
A way around! But one which will avert
My suffering any losses, if you please—!
Oh, stop it! Put this ugliness aside!

(Takes a few steps toward the cabin, then stops)

Go in like this? In so debased a state?
Weighed down with witchcraft? To communicate,
But keep my secrets—to confess, but hide—?

(Throws the axe down)

To so profane the holy privilege

She offers me would be a sacrilege!

SOLVEIG *(In the doorway)*:

Coming?

PEER GYNT *(In a whisper)*:

Around!

SOLVEIG:

What's that?

PEER GYNT:

You'll have to wait!

This is a heavy load—it's getting late!

SOLVEIG:

I'll help! Now you're no longer on your own!

PEER GYNT:

Stay there! I have to carry it alone!

SOLVEIG:

Will it take long?

PEER GYNT:

I might be late.

Be patient, girl—and wait.

SOLVEIG *(Nodding as he leaves)*:

I'll wait!

(Peer Gynt walks toward the forest path. Solveig remains behind the open Dutch door)

Aase's cottage. Evening. Logs are burning, casting light on the chimney. The cat on a stool by the foot of the bed. Aase is in bed, fumbling restlessly with the blanket.

AASE:

> When is he coming? God Almighty!
> I think there must be something wrong
> With him. Should he not come tonight, he
> Will have remained away too long.
> So little time—and me so sickly!
> With still two things I'd like to know—
> How did time pass me by so quickly?
> Also—was I too hard on him or no?

PEER GYNT *(Comes in)*:

> Hello!

AASE:

> God bless and keep you, Peer, dear!
> So, child, you made it after all!
> How dare you? What if you were snared here?
> Your life's at stake! What might befall
> My boy if they—

PEER GYNT:

> I don't care, mother!
> Had I not come, would I deserve to live?

AASE:

> Now I can pass on to the other
> World in peace. I will not forgive
> That Kari doubting you, though!

PEER GYNT:

> You were saying
> You think you have someplace to go?

AASE:

> I fear it's over, Peer! You should start praying
> For me! My hours here below
> Are running out.

PEER GYNT *(Turns away and paces the floor)*:

> Mother, I was hoping

Here I'd be free of difficult
Problems—let's talk now; no more moping!
AASE:

It's over, Peer! You're an adult
Now—act your age! When you determine
My eyes aren't moving, close them carefully.
Construct a box that keeps the vermin
Out, but is also handsome. Oh, dear me!
Of course—you can't!
PEER GYNT:

                                    Quiet! There's plenty
Of time tomorrow—no more of that today.
AASE *(Agitated, looking around the room)*:

There's nothing left. Oh, what a gent he
Was—Haegstad! As he took it all away!
PEER GYNT *(Turning around)*:

Mother, again!

(Harshly)

                        Must you repeat it
Over and over? I know that I'm to blame!
AASE:

You're not the first to be defeated,
And made unhappy—burdened with lasting shame—
By devil drink. You weren't in your senses
That night—that's all!—and so you ran amok,
Dizzy—I know!—from jumping over fences,
Riding high across the sky on that big buck.
PEER GYNT:

Yes, yes—well, let's forget that story.
In fact, forget the whole damn thing!
Everything's fine—it's hunky-dory!
Difficult things we're tabling

Until tomorrow!

(Sits on the edge of the bed)

           Let's have a discussion,
But only small talk, mother, please!
Let's choose a subject free of repercussion
Or painful, bitter memories.
Look at that cat! This is a sight I'm
Going to treasure! Still alive!

AASE:

Oh, how he carries on at nighttime!
You know what that means, don't you—I've—

PEER GYNT *(Changing the subject)*:

Give me some news about the valley.

AASE *(Smiling)*:

They say a girl is woebegone—
Her spirits never seem to rally—

PEER GYNT *(Interrupting)*:

Mads Moen—how's he getting on?

AASE:

They say the pain and lamentation
Of that girl's parents fall on stone-deaf ears.
You could give her gratification—
Peer, pay a visit, and some of your arrears—

PEER GYNT:

And how about that blacksmith fellow?

AASE:

Shut up about that dirty brute!
Why don't we talk about more mellow
Things, like that girl—you can't dispute—

PEER GYNT:

No, mother! Let's have a discussion,
But only small talk—pretty please!

A subject free of repercussion
Or painful, bitter memories.
Thirsty? I'm sure you should be drinking
Something! Can you stretch out? This bed's so small.
Let me see—just what I was thinking!
This bed was mine when I could barely crawl!
Remember how you'd say, "This is the right time
For you to sleep, now close your eyes!"
You'd tuck me in, and well into the nighttime,
You'd sing me songs and lullabies.

AASE:

And we played horse and sleigh—do you remember—
When father was away? Outside, the storm!
The floor—a fjord sparkling with December
Ice—and this blanket was what kept us warm.

PEER GYNT:

Oh, yes, mother—but what was even better—
Can you remember?—it's so long ago!—
Was Blackie, the skittish horse—our best pacesetter.

AASE:

But do you really think I wouldn't know?
Perched on the stool, our horse was Kari's kitten—
Oh, he was fast, he couldn't be outrun—

PEER GYNT:

Our castle shamed those little things in Britain—
Mother, let's go there now! East of the sun,
West of the moon, the Soria-Moria castle!
The road demands some horsemanship!
We took a walking stick, tied on a tassel—
And that became our riding whip!

AASE:

I stood in front, doing the driving—

PEER GYNT:

    And you'd let go the reins—oh, you were bold!—
    To see if I were still surviving,
    And ask so graciously if I were cold.
    God bless you! What an ugly flyblown
    Terror you were—but so solicitous—
    Why did you groan?

AASE:

                  God, my old, dry bones
    Against these boards—it's downright treacherous!

PEER GYNT:

    Stretch out! Those poor old bones are showing
    Their age, that's all. That's better, right? Now, then!

AASE *(Agitated)*:

    Oh, Peer, thank God I'm going!

PEER GYNT:

                  Going?

AASE:

    Yes, going, Peer! Over and over again
    I've wished for it.

PEER GYNT:

              Oh, you're just talking
    Nonsense! Now I want you to close your eyes,
    And I'll be here to hold you, rocking
    You off to sleep with songs and lullabies.

AASE:

    The Book of Homilies is in the closet.
    Get it, please. It will lend me peace of mind.

PEER GYNT:

    Get in the sleigh! I'm going to deposit
    You at a party. All of the refined
    Folk of the Soria-Moria castle will be
    Present. Relax now; it's a long, long ride—

AASE:

But Peer, am I invited?

PEER GYNT:

Don't be silly!
We both are! It would be undignified
To go, otherwise!

(Throws a string over the chair where the cat is lying, picks up a stick, and sits on the foot of the bed)

Giddyup now, Blackie!
You'll tell me if you're chilly, right?
Mother, see that!—the sweat on Blackie's back?—he
Really likes cantering tonight!

AASE:

Peer, what is that? I hear a clinging
Sound—!

PEER GYNT:

It's the harness bells, my dear!

AASE:

Oh, no! It's such a hollow ringing!

PEER GYNT:

We're on the fjord now—please don't interfere!

AASE:

Peer, I'm afraid! What are those yowling
And moaning sounds? They seem so strange and wild!

PEER GYNT:

Mother, it's only wind. It's howling
Through the blue spruces on the moor.

AASE:

But child,

What's sparkling and flashing in the distance?
Where does that light come from?

PEER GYNT:

It's all
From windows in the castle. Your assistance
Has been requested at the ball.

AASE:

Really?

PEER GYNT:

And outside stands St. Peter
Inviting you to come inside.

AASE:

Me?

PEER GYNT:

Yes! He's offering us a liter
Of wine! The best I've ever tried!

AASE:

Wine—goodness! Does he also have some pastries?

PEER GYNT:

Of course! A tray filled to the brink.
And now—just watch—the pastor's wife will say,
"Please,
Won't you come in for food and drink?"

AASE:

Oh, my! Not she and I together!

PEER GYNT:

As much as you would like to be.

AASE:

Peer, what a party! It's a feather
In the cap for an old thing like me!

PEER GYNT *(Using the whip)*:

Giddyup, Blackie! Hurry! Come, now!

AASE:

This is the right direction, Peer?

PEER GYNT *(Using the whip again)*:

The road is wide and smooth here.

AASE:

Somehow

The ride is more than I can bear.

PEER GYNT:

The journey's almost over, mother.

I see the castle up above.

AASE:

I'll close my eyes for just another

Moment till we arrive, my love!

PEER GYNT:

Hurry up, Blackie, you old critter!

Look at the crowds around the castle gate—

Swarming about—torches aglitter!

Peer and his mom have come! Let's celebrate!

St. Peter what? What's that he's saying?

St. Peter says he won't let mother in?

You tell him he will be surveying

Mankind a long time till he finds a skin

Honest as hers! Now I'm not talking

About myself! I'll turn around right now—

Don't say a word! I'll just start walking—

Though offering me a drink, you must allow,

Would not be inappropriate. The devil

In the pulpit hasn't lied as much as I,

I know! Yes, I've descended to the level

Of calling her a hen—I made her cry!—

Because she squawked so much. But thou shalt honor

My mother; thou shalt treat her right!

Lavish respect and compliments upon her—

Her better won't be found tonight.
Ho-ho, St. Peter, here comes God the Father!
I think he'll make you see what's what!

(In a deep voice)

"Why are you being so officious! Don't bother
Her—she comes in, like it or not!"

(Laughs out loud and turns around to his mother)

Now *that's* a bird of a different feather!
Didn't I say how it would be?

(Uneasily)

Please look at me! I can't tell whether—
Don't! You're behaving foolishly!

(Goes to the head of the bed)

Say something! No! That's not what I intended!
It's Peer! Mother, you're staring into space!

*(Gently feels her forehead and hands, then he throws the string on
the chair and says in a low voice)*

Well, Blackie, finally the journey's ended;
Now you can stop. We've reached our resting place.

(Closes her eyes and bends over her)

Thanks for each lullaby, thanks for each spanking;
Thank you, my dear, for every livelong day.
Well, come on, don't you think you should be thanking
Me in return?

(Puts his cheek against her mouth)

                There, that's the driver's pay.

KARI *(Coming in)*:

What—Peer! You've come! Oh, good! Her deepest sorrow
Was not having her son beside her bed.
She looks like she could sleep until tomorrow,
Or is she—Oh, God!

PEER GYNT:

                     Shh! She's gone. She's dead.

*(Kari cries over the body. Peer Gynt walks around the room for a
long time; finally, he stops beside the bed)*

Bury her soon, with proper devotion.
I have to go now! Kari—do you hear?

KARI:

You're going far?

PEER GYNT:

                     Across the ocean.

KARI:

So far?

PEER GYNT:

               As far as I can go from here!

(He goes)

Act Four

On the southwest coast of Morocco. A palm grove. A table set for dinner, an awning and a reed mat. Some hammocks are suspended farther into the grove. Offshore is a power yacht showing Norwegian and American flags. On the beach is a dinghy. It is close to sunset.

Peer Gynt, a good-looking, middle-aged gentleman in an elegant traveling suit, a gold pince-nez on his chest, presides as the host at the head of the table. Master Cotton, Monsieur Ballon as well as Messrs. von Eberkopf[13] and Trumpeterstraale[14] are in the process of finishing the meal.

PEER GYNT:

> Gentlemen, drink! If we're created
> For pleasure, please yourselves and seize the day.
> What's lost is lost, as it's been stated,
> Gone's gone! How would you like some Chardonnay?

TRUMPETERSTRAALE:

> My brother Gynt, you are the perfect host!

PEER GYNT:

> Please! You should praise my butler and my cook.

I provide nothing but the pocketbook.

MASTER COTTON:

Very well! To the three of you! A toast!

MONSIEUR BALLON:

Monsieur, you have a *gout*, a *ton*,
And seldom is it found today
Among men living *en garcon*—
I don't know how—

VON EBERKOPF:

He is endowed
With free spiritual association
And cosmopolitan administration.
He pierces through the rent in the cloud,
Unfettered by what people say,
To arrive at reason's highest sphere. We sense
An ancient nature with experience
And the integrity of Holy Trinity.
Monsieur, that's more or less—*nien?*—the vicinity
Of your intent?

MONSIEUR BALLON:

Yes, but it may
Not sound so graceful *en francais*!

VON EBERKOPF:

Ei was! That language is so ordinary!
To understand you better, and satisfy
Our curiosity—

PEER GYNT:

I'll tell you why—
Because I've not allowed myself to marry.
Yes, gentlemen, this is quite clearly
The thing—a man must be himself alone!
Himself! I can't speak more sincerely.
Cherish *yourself* and *everything you own*!

But can a beast that's burdened by a clan—
And obligations—follow such a plan?

VON EBERKOPF:

But, sir, this for-and-by-yourself ontology
Must once have cost you dearly, no?

PEER GYNT:

Certainly, yes—long, long ago.
But I prevailed, and I make no apology.
Against my will, I once came all too close
To being trapped in domesticity.
I was a bright good-looking lad.
The cherished lass with all the grandiose
Plans had, of course, a royal family tree—

MONSIEUR BALLON:

Of royal blood?

PEER GYNT *(Casually)*:

               The father's side.

TRUMPETERSTRAALE *(Hitting his fist on the table)*:

These highborn trolls! I get so mad—

PEER GYNT *(Shrugging his shoulders)*:

The aristocracy takes pride
In keeping commoners a wide
Wide world away from their own coat-of-arms!

MASTER COTTON:

But you did not succumb to all her charms?

MONSIEUR BALLON:

The family of the bride disliked the match?

PEER GYNT:

No, not at all.

MONSIEUR BALLON:

           Aha!

PEER GYNT *(Gently)*:

              But one or more

Things indicated we should wed before
One of the indicators chanced to hatch.
It all repelled me, to be frank,
From the beginning to the very end.
I'm fussy, yes, but this was rank.
I'm sure you gentlemen can comprehend.
Father-in-law-to-be was making
Certain demands that set me shaking
With fury—change my name and loyalty,
File applications for the royalty—
It truly was unappetizing,
Not to mention compromising.
I withdrew firmly and politely
And brushed aside his ultimatums,
Surrendering my bride contritely.

(Drumming on the table, piously)

Well, well—as always, that's where Fate comes
In to tell man what he should most rely on,
Reminding us that bygones shall be bygone.

MONSIEUR BALLON:

The matter was allowed to die?

PEER GYNT:

No, it went on and on! It truly was amazing!
Some busybodies got involved, and started raising
A stupefying hue and cry.
The youngsters of the family were the worst—
I duelled seven of the brood, no less.
I thought—during that time—that I was cursed,
Though, finally, I enjoyed a great success.
Blood always tells, and blood was shed
That told my foes my value and my rate.
It shows the wisdom, as I've said,

Of trusting in the guiding hand of Fate.

VON EBERKOPF:

You have a world view that's unique
And elevates you to the peak
Of wisdom. Others only have opinions
On this and that; they're bound by the dominions
Of eye and ear. That's merely apprehension!
But you are blessed with *total* comprehension!
Using a single standard in all cases,
You focus your deliberation!
Opinions and conclusions then have basis,
Thanks to your lifelong cerebration.
You've had no formal education?

PEER GYNT:

It is enough to be—I thought
I'd made the point before—self-taught.
I haven't learned a thing methodically.
I've thought, and practiced contemplation,
And read, and now I'm almost scholarly.
I wasn't young when I got started,
And I was nearly brokenhearted
Plowing again and again through endless pages,
Progressing in what seemed like tiny stages.
I learned my history in bits and pieces—
Believe me, all the time I had I used—
And when one comes upon hard times—well, then
One must believe in something, so I perused
Religious texts—quite slowly—it decreases
Consumption but improves digestion. When
Reading, be careful what you swallow
And only seek what you can follow—

MASTER COTTON:

That's awfully practical!

PEER GYNT *(Lights a cigar)*:
>My friends,
Think about how my life's progressed.
What was I when I first went West!
A fellow without means or ends!
I earned my daily bread! I was no quitter!
Believe me, it was no mean feat.
But life—no matter what—is sweet,
And death, they say—I wouldn't know—is bitter.
As you know, Lady Luck was good to me,
And old man Fate provided bountifully—
I thrived. But, in reality, who could be
Much more deserving? Things got better and better.
The Charlestown merchants in those golden years
Nicknamed me Croesus; each one was my debtor,
And they spread my fame throughout both hemispheres.
I had a fortune in my hold—

MASTER COTTON:
What was your business, sir?

PEER GYNT:
>I sold
Two items—Negroes in Carolina
And heathen images to China.

MONSIEUR BALLON:
Fi donc!

TRUMPETERSTRAALE:
>*Foer tusan*,[15] my dear Gynt!

PEER GYNT:
It's wrong, you think? At least a gray
Area, no? It makes you squint!
Of course, you're right—Feel the same way
Myself! Yes, I too found it odious.

But it's not easy to obey
Your conscience when it's incommodious.
In such a mighty enterprise—
Thousands of employees, their families—
Cutting it off presents difficulties
And can be cruel, if not unwise.
"Cutting it off!" No, I can't stand
The thought. But on the other hand
I've always had profound respect
For what are usually called the consequences,
And since excess, God knows, only incenses
Folk, I thought I'd be circumspect.
And I was getting old; my youth had fled.
Fifty! You know what that connotes.
My hair was slowly turning gray,
And though my health was excellent,
One thought caused me some discontent—
Who knows for sure his final day?
Or when the jury's verdict will be read
That separates the sheep from goats?
What could I do? To stop the trade
To China wasn't practical or wise!
I found an answer—I parlayed
My business into one that would neutralize
The bad effects. In Spring I shipped the beasts
False idols, and in the Fall I sent them priests—
Providing them with all the necessaries
Like socks and bibles, rice, a little rum—

MASTER COTTON:

Sure, at a profit!

PEER GYNT:

Oh, a tidy sum!

The business worked this way—the missionaries
Made certain that for every god
I sold, they had a coolie nod
His head and find the grace of true baptism.
The mission's work—it never ceased!
Each dollar that I made from paganism
Gave full employment to a priest.

MASTER COTTON:

Well, I'll be—what about the Negro freight?

PEER GYNT:

Morality won *that* round, too.
I knew the time was overdue—
Considering my age—for my retirement
From such a trade. Who knows what the requirement
Is, after all, to pass the pearly gate?
Besides, philanthropists were setting traps;
You never know where pirates lie in wait
To rob you; weather caused a few mishaps;
So I took stock, and thought, "Now, Peer, perhaps
The time has come to trim your sails,
Correct your mistakes, balance the scales."
I made the purchase of an old plantation
Down South, kept for myself the final shipment
Of flesh, and let me tell you, choice equipment
It was—so shiny, fat and happy—
Ready to smile—they called me pappy!
In fact, without the slightest reservation
I honestly can say I was a father
To them. They were investments, not a bother
After all. I built them schools—for education,
I'm sure you know already, helps maintain
Virtue on an accepted social plane.
I used my own thermometer to see

That temperatures stayed near the right degree.
However, I've now pulled up stakes
From those parts. Wary of the peril
To my soul, and fearful of mistakes,
I sold the farm—lock, stock and barrel.
But even as I left, I recall
How I gave whisky—free!—to one and all—
(Snuff to the widows)—along with my goodbye,
So that, in parting, spirits were quite high.
Someone has said—by God, I hope it's true,
For words can sometimes be misunderstood—
That if you've not done bad, then you've done good.
If so, my sins are really very few.
And unlike most men—it is downright nice
To say—my virtue far outweighs my vice.

VON EBERKOPF *(Clinking glasses with him)*:
How invigorating, sir, it is to hear
Some basic principles put center stage,
Delivered from the darkness of this age,
The night of theory, forthright and sincere!

PEER GYNT *(Who has been working heavily on the bottle during the foregoing)*:
We northern gentlemen know how to wage
A battle. Friends, without a doubt,
The art of living is to never hear
The serpent speak! To bolt and latch your ear
And keep the little devil out!

MASTER COTTON:
What kind of serpent, my rich friend?

PEER GYNT:

                A queer
Deceitful pest who will seduce a man
Into the folly of a master plan

That can't be changed.

(Drinks again)

                                   The "art of enterprise"
Means that you must possess the will to do—
Ready for action! And never should you
Be cornered. You must always realize
That each day need not end in battle—
The most important thing's to win the war!
And never should you burn a bridge before
You retreat. Friends, this isn't prattle!
These principles have got me where I am,
And they have colored my whole personality.
Though some might criticize them for banality,
They're my inheritance, my monogram!
MONSIEUR BALLON:
    You are Norwegian, right?
PEER GYNT:

                                   Only by birth—
Citizen of the world by temperament!
America can claim my sentiment
Because she made of me a man of worth.
From Germany—the new philosophy—
Came my world view, and my theosophy.
From France I get my clothes, my cook,
Also a certain flair for fashion;
From England comes the sense to look
Out for yourself, and a passion
For hard work. Jews taught me to wait,
And I picked up a little trait
Of *dolce far niente* when
I was in Italy. And then

There was the time I made a better deal
With the support of sturdy Swedish steel.
TRUMPETERSTRAALE *(Raising his glass)*:
    To Swedish steel!
VON EBERKOPF:
                        My friends, a toast
To Swedish steel and to our host!

(They clink glasses and drink. Peer Gynt is beginning to get light-headed)

MASTER COTTON:
    All well and good; you needn't sell us
    On all your virtues—we'd like to be told
    Sir, what you plan to do with all your gold.
PEER GYNT *(Smiling)*:
    Hmmm! Do? Really?
ALL FOUR *(Moving closer)*:
                        Yes, yes! Please tell us!
PEER GYNT:
    Well, first of all, I'd like to travel.
    I chose you four as shipmates in Gibraltar
    To provide camaraderie—
    There should be chorus boys around the altar
    Of the golden calf, don't you agree?
VON EBERKOPF:
    How clever!
MASTER COTTON:
                    I don't like to cavil,
    But no one sails only for sailing's sake.
    They have a motive—let's make no mistake.
    What's yours?
PEER GYNT:
            To be emperor.

ALL FOUR:

Hee!

What?

PEER GYNT *(Nodding)*:

Emperor!

ALL FOUR:

Where?

PEER GYNT:

Everywhere!

MONSIEUR BALLON:

How—?

PEER GYNT:

By the power, friend, of cash!
Of gold! It's not a new idea of mine;
I've mentioned it in every prayer
Since childhood when, in dreams, I'd flash
Around the world to Spain, or Palestine,
My golden train billowing into space—
True, I was always falling on my face,
But that did not affect my motivation.
I don't remember the exact location,
But it's been written, or someone has stated,
That even if you won the world, but lost
Yourself, the crown you purchased at such cost
Surrounds a temple that's been devastated.
Or thereabouts—this is from memory—
Believe me, those words are not just poetry!

VON EBERKOPF:

This Gyntian *self*—what is it, anyhow?

PEER GYNT:

Everything that lies behind my brow
That sets Peer Gynt apart from you,
As far as God from You-Know-Who.

TRUMPETERSTRAALE:

Eureka! That's where this is going! Now I see!

MONSIEUR BALLON:

Sublime philosophy!

VON EBERKOPF:

And noble poetry!

PEER GYNT *(More and more lightheaded)*:

The Gyntian *self*—I'll tell you what that comprehends—
An army of desires, wishes, claims that never ends!
The Gyntian self—it is a teeming flood
Of needs, ideas and wants—it's the life blood,
In brief, raising and lowering my chest
And making my existence manifest.
But God, you know, needed some dust—
Yes, dust!—in order to create us;
And I must have some gold—I must!—
If I'm to gain imperial status.

MONSIEUR BALLON:

But you have gold already!

PEER GYNT:

Yes, enough
For two or three acres or so,
For Lichtenstein or Monaco!
To be myself, with no fear of rebuff,
Then I must Gynt the universe!
Lord Gynt—for better or for worse!

MONSIEUR BALLON *(Getting carried away)*:

To own the world in all of its great wonders!

VON EBERKOPF:

Johannisberger wine from every single year!

TRUMPETERSTRAALE:

The armory of Charles the Twelfth[16]—each sword, each
spear!

MASTER COTTON:

But first let's talk about a little plunder—

PEER GYNT:

My friend, I'm way ahead of you.
An explanation's overdue.
Tonight our ship heads north. Excuse
Me for not telling you the news
Sooner, but I myself found out today.

(Stands and raises his glass)

My friends—I'd rather not be Machiavellian,
But—luck helps those who help themselves, they say—

ALL FOUR:

What happened? Well?

PEER GYNT:

The Greeks are in rebellion.

ALL FOUR *(Jumping to their feet)*:

What's that? The Greeks—?

PEER GYNT:

Have risen up in arms.

ALL FOUR:

Hooray!

PEER GYNT:

The Turks are sounding the alarms!

(Empties his glass)

MONSIEUR BALLON:

To Greece, where I will fight with pride!
The gate of honor opens wide!

VON EBERKOPF:

And I'll be cheering—on the side; ballistics
Is not my forte!

MASTER COTTON:

And I'll help with logistics.

TRUMPETERSTRAALE:

Let's go! In Bender[17] I perhaps

Can find the famous leather straps![18]

MONSIEUR BALLON *(Embracing Peer Gynt)*:

Forgive me, friend, that I should ever err

By doubting you!

VON EBERKOPF *(Shaking his hand)*:

And I—a stupid cur—

Thought you were nothing but a reprobate!

MASTER COTTON:

Oh, that's too strong—a little less than ample

Sense, perhaps—

TRUMPETERSTRAALE *(About to kiss him)*:

I had thought you an example

Of what those Yankee brutes can procreate!

Forgive me, dearest sir!

VON EBERKOPF:

We've all been blind!

PEER GYNT:

What's this about?

VON EBERKOPF:

We see what is behind

This army of desires—these never ending

Wishes and claims! Now we are comprehending!

MONSIEUR BALLON *(Admiringly)*:

So *that's* the Monsieur Gynt you want to be!

VON EBERKOPF *(The same)*:

Now *that* is being Gynt honorably!

PEER GYNT:

But tell me—?

MONSIEUR BALLON:

>   Don't you understand?

PEER GYNT:

>   Damned if I do! There's something very funny—!

MONSIEUR BALLON:

>   Aren't you going to lend a hand

>   To help the Greek cause with your ship and money?

PEER GYNT *(Blows through his lips)*:

>   No thanks! I'm not that full of quirks;

>   I'll lend my money to the Turks.

MONSIEUR BALLON:

>   Impossible!

VON EBERKOPF:

>   A funny joke!

PEER GYNT *(Falls silent for a moment, leans on the chair, and assumes a worldly-wise demeanor)*:

>   Listen, my friends, I think it's best

>   We separate before the rest

>   Of our good feelings fade like smoke.

>   The man who doesn't own a thing can breezily

>   Make promises. If you're the kind of plodder

>   Who owns nothing but his shadow, I can easily

>   See why you're dying to be cannon fodder.

>   But if you stand above the common herd,

>   As I do, such a gesture is absurd.

>   Gentlemen, go to Athens! Go!

>   I'll send you men and weapons, gratis!

>   The more widespread the combat is,

>   The tighter I can string the bow.

>   Fight nobly! Fight for freedom and for right!

>   Fight up a storm! And give the Turks a fright!

>   And even though you're bound to be a goner

>   On a Janissary's[19] lance, you'll go with honor!

But count me out! I am myself—Sir Peter Gynt;

(Pats his pocket)

I'm worth too much to risk it in a hail of flint!

(He opens his umbrella and walks into the grove, where the hammocks are barely visible)

TRUMPETERSTRAALE:
That pig!
MONSIEUR BALLON:
No sense of honor!
MASTER COTTON:
Drat!
To hell with honor—who needs that!—
But what financial opportunity—
Imagine!—In the name of liberty!
MONSIEUR BALLON:
I saw myself as a victorious hero
Surrounded by Greek dancing girls! Oh, dear, oh
Dear, oh dear!
TRUMPETERSTRAALE:
But if this should all collapse,
I'll lose my chance to get the leather straps!
VON EBERKOPF:
I saw the perfect moment to expand
The domination of the fatherland!
MASTER COTTON:
The disadvantage, friends, is more concrete!
Goddammit—I could cry! Let me repeat
It for you—money! We could own
Olympus, gentlemen! The excavation
Of minerals—copper alone!—
Would make us magnates—if her reputation

Is true. And then there's talk about a river—
Castale, I think—that they say can deliver
Thousands and thousands of kilowatts per hour
With all its waterfalls—that's hydropower—!

TRUMPETERSTRAALE:

My Swedish sword cannot be sold
For all his filthy Yankee gold!
I'm going!

MASTER COTTON:

            But that's asinine
If all we do is stand in line.
Everyone else looking to make a buck
Will be there, too.

MONSIEUR BALLON:

            The peak of happiness
Was near; now we are at the grave! What luck!

MASTER COTTON *(Shaking his clenched fist at the ship)*:

That goddam pitch-black box of nastiness
Holds all the gold that nabob sweated out of Negroes!

VON EBERKOPF:

A thought that's worthy of a Romanov!
His empire soon will be the patches on his elbows!
Hooray!

MONSIEUR BALLON:

           What do you mean?

VON EBERKOPF:

              Quick! We'll buy off
The crew without the slightest trouble,
And seize the vessel! On the double!

MASTER COTTON:

You—what—?

VON EBERKOPF:

           We must move quickly! Come!

(Walks toward the dinghy)

MASTER COTTON:
> My conscience tells me I can't let him
> Do it alone.

(Follows along)

TRUMPETERSTRAALE:
> We can't abet him!

MONSIEUR BALLON:
> Disgusting, but. . . . *Enfin*! Succumb
> I must!

(Follows the others)

TRUMPETERSTRAALE:
> I must go with the other three,
> But I'm protesting, as you all can see!

(Follows them)

Another spot on the beach. Moonlight and passing clouds. The yacht is in the distance, pulling away at full speed. Peer Gynt is running along the beach. Alternately pinching his arms, and looking out toward the ocean.

PEER GYNT:
> A nightmare! Foolishness! I'll wake up soon!
> It's pulling out—I think I'm going to swoon!
> It's picked up speed. It's foolishness! I'm high!
> Asleep!

(Wrings his hands)

They couldn't leave me here to die!

(Tears his hair)

A dream! I want it, please, to be a dream!
It's tragic! But it's true—they're all aboard!
My goddam friends! Listen to me, oh Lord!

(With his arms raised to the sky)

So wise and fair! All-powerful, supreme!
It's *me*, remember, Peter Gynt? Protect me,
Father, watch over me; if you reject me,
It's curtains! Stop those thieves! Do something to the rig!
Make them back up the engines! Throw them in the brig!
Listen to me! Let other people go!
Let them care for themselves a while! Hello!
He doesn't hear! Of course not—God is deaf!
Whenever I'm in need, He peters out!

(Waves to the sky)

Psst! All the slaves are gone—except my chef—
Those missionaries? Wasn't that devout?
Come on, I've scratched your back, now you scratch mine!
Help me!

(Flame and heavy smoke billow from the yacht; a hollow explosion follows; Peer Gynt cries out, and collapses on the sand; gradually the smoke disappears; there is no sign of the ship. Peer Gynt continues, pale, soft-spoken)

The sword of righteousness! Divine
Punishment—to the bottom with a plop!
Lord, thank you! What a stroke of luck! No, stop!

(Emotionally)

A stroke of luck? It's more than that.

I'm saved, they're not. *Requiescat*
In pace! Thank you, Lord, for your protection!
You keep an eye on me despite my flaws—

(Lets out a sigh)

It is a sobering thought—it gives me pause—
That I'm the object of divine affection.
The desert! How will I get food and drink?
He knows that! I'll find what I need, won't I?
It's not so bad!

(In a loud, ingratiating voice)

　　　　　　　He certainly would think
Of that! His little sparrow wouldn't die!
Be humble—put your faith in God above,
And He'll provide, if push should come to shove.

(Jumps in fright)

Was that a lion roaring in the brush?

(With chattering teeth)

A lion!

(Pulls himself together)

　　　　　　　I can say with some insistence—
Those beasts, they know enough to keep their distance.
They never trifle with their betters. Hush!
Instinct will keep them from performing stunts
Like that—to play around with elephants.
Still, maybe I should try to find a tree.
There are a few acacias and some palms;
Above, I might find some security—
And more so if I could recall some psalms—

(Climbs up)

They say that morning isn't like the night,
And sure enough, it's just as we were taught.

(Makes himself comfortable)

How wonderful to know you've seen the light.
Thinking of money's not the only thought,
You know, that's noble! Trust in Him, for He
Knows how much pain and suffering to allot.
We have a special cordiality;

(Throws a glance at the ocean, and whispers, with a sigh)

But economical—that he is not!

Night. A Moroccan camp on the edge of the desert. Campfire and mounted soldiers, resting.

A SLAVE *(Running in, pulling his hair)*:
    The emperor's white horse is gone!
SECOND SLAVE *(Tearing his clothes as he runs in)*:
    They took the emperor's kerchief!
SLAVE MASTER *(Coming in)*:
    A hundred thousand lashes on
    Each one who doesn't catch the thief!

(The soldiers jump on horseback and gallop off in all directions)

Dawn. The grove of acacias and palms. Peer Gynt in a tree holding a branch he has broken off, fighting for his life with a group of monkeys.

PEER GYNT:

Damn you! This was a most distressing way
To spend the night!

(Waves his arms around)

Great, now they're throwing fruit!
Oh, no—it's something else. You filthy brute!
A monkey's not a pleasant beast! Touché!
It's written: you must stay on guard and fight,
But I'm too tired to keep this up all day.

(He's attacked again; he becomes impatient)

What can I do to drive them all away?
I have to catch one of these impolite
Bastards; I'll draw and quarter him, and then
Dress in his shaggy hide—the others might
Foolishly think that I am genuine.
What is this thing called man! He's just a speck.
And when in Rome, you know what you must do—
Still more! They're underfoot, around my neck!
Get out! What's making them so frantic? Shoo!
What can I use to make a phony tail?
If I can pass for one of them, then they'll—
What's that! Another one is up above—

(Looks up)

The old one—with his hands chock full of dirt—!

(Curls up apprehensively and doesn't move for a moment. The monkey makes a movement; Peer Gynt tries to relax and sweet-talk him with a friendly tone, as if he were talking to a dog)

Hey, Boog! Good Boog! Oh, no! He wouldn't hurt
His friend! He only wants a little love,
Isn't that right? He wouldn't throw that, would he?
It's me! Uk-uk! Yes, there's no need to fight!
Hu-hu! Hu-hu! I speak your language, right?
Are you my cousin, Boog? You know, you could be.
I might give Boog some sugar and—! Dag nab it!
All over me! Oh, no! Oh, God, it's hideous!
Or is it food? The taste is—well!—ambiguous;
And as for taste, the crucial thing is habit.
Who was the great philosopher who said,
"Spit, and hope habit will enhance the taste?"
The brutes are back!

(Striking out and defending himself)

                    It is a dreadful waste
For man to battle with a quadruped—
Man should be master of the universe—
My God! The old one's bad, but the young are worse!

Early morning. Rocky terrain on the edge of the desert. On one side, a cave and a ravine. A thief and a fence are in front of the cave with the emperor's horse and clothing. The horse is richly saddled, tied to a rock. Mounted warriors in the distance.

THIEF:

The lance's tongue
It gleams, it plays—
You see, you see?

FENCE:

> My head and I
> Will soon part ways!
> Oh, me—oh, me!

THIEF *(Folds his arms over his chest)*:

> My father's a thief;
> So I have to rob.

FENCE:

> My father's a fence;
> I have the same job.

THIEF:

> You are who you are;
> Yourself you must be.

FENCE *(Listening)*:

> I hear them in the brush!
> Let's beat it! Fast and far!

THIEF:

> The cave is dark and deep—
> Allah be good to me!

(They run away and leave the stolen property behind. Warriors in the distance)

PEER GYNT *(Comes in, cutting a reed pipe)*:

> Life in the morning—what a state of grace!
> The scarab rolls away his ball of dirt,
> The snail creeps from his shell—alive, unhurt.
> The morning—yes!—gold shining from its face!
> Is nature not possessed of foresight
> To give such energy to daylight?
> I feel so safe, and so courageous, so full
> Of strength. I think that I could fight a bull.
> How still and peaceful! Ah, the country joys!
> I was a fool to sneer at them before—

For what? To hang around with city boys—
Those bums—who show the likes of me the door?
Look how four-legged creatures run around
Thinking of nothing, noses to the ground!
Animals! They have true naivete.
They follow the Commandments carefully,
To God and nature true eternally.
They are themselves at work or play,
Themselves as on the very first day.

(Puts his pince-nez on his nose)

A toad. Caught in a tiny sandstone bluff,
Encased by rock. We see his head alone.
He peers at us through windowpanes of stone
Saying, "To mine own self I'm true enough!"

(Thinks for a moment)

Enough? Myself? Wonder who wrote that stuff?
I read it as a boy—ah, life's anomalies—
In some great book. The Good Book? The Book of
                              Homilies?
Now here's a morbid notion—as the years
Go by, it seems my memory disappears.

(Sits down in the shade)

It's cool here. Rest and stretch your feet. Incredible!
Look at the ferns; they're no doubt edible.

(Takes a taste)

If you fed this to cows, you would get bitten!
Nature obeys necessity—it's written—
As well as, if you're snooty, you will fall,
And he who's last shall rise above them all.

(Disturbed)

Rise? Why not me? Why not today!
What else is possible? You understand?
Fate will arrange that I escape this land;
She'll pick me up and fly away.
This is a trial. Soon I'll be saved—and wealthy—
If the Good Lord allows me to stay healthy.

(Pushes the thought away, lights a cigar, stretches, and gazes into the desert)

Limitless waste and blazing skies!
On the horizon, I can see an ostrich!
Can anybody say precisely what niche
In God's plan this place occupies?
Life has been burned away by too much sun.
It gives no benefits to anyone.
This piece of earth, forever fallow,
Since the creation it has not been tasteful
Enough to give to God a sallow
Thank you. Wherefore does it exist? It's wasteful!
Is that the ocean in the east, twinkling rills
Of motion? No, that's an illusion.
The ocean's west, and this protrusion
Of desert's here because of all those rolling hills

(A thought strikes him)

Holding back—A canal! A narrow ridge
Holding back water! Move the hill a smidge
And water rushes through the channel, floods
The desert, bringing life! Creating buds!
Soon all this smoldering waste will be
As fertile as the shining sea.
Yes, lush oases rise like islands.
The Atlas will be northern green, not tan.
Sailors will float over the highlands

Across the traces of the caravan.
These noxious fumes will be dispersed
By air that's fresh, and grass will grow beneath the palm.
Town after town will rise with majesty and calm
And dew will slake the flowers' thirst.
Lands to the south, Sahara's neighbors,
Will learn the sea and its new labors.
Through Ethiopia, by Pullman car, a team
Of scientists will travel to the Upper Nile.
The factories of Timbuktu will run on steam,
And Borneo vacations—that will be the style.
My ocean round me, on a huge oasis,
I'll plant the seed of the Norwegian races.
My northern blood is close to being blue—
As for the rest, Arabic genes will do.
Within a crescent cove, perched on a sandy beach,
I'll build a thriving new metropolis.
Out with the Old World!

(Jumps up)

To Peeropolis!
And my new nation, Gyntiana! Speech, speech, speech!
Money is all I need! The golden key
That opens up the gateway to the sea!
Yes, a crusade against the desert! Misers
Will raid their vaults, becoming sympathizers
In the great cause! Everyone, everywhere will join!
Just like the ass aboard the ark, I'll send
A shout to slaves around the world and lend
My voice to freedom! Freedom! That's the golden coin!
I must get going! Gyntianas west and east!
My kingdom for a horse! Well, half of it at least.

(From a cave, a horse neighs)

A horse! And armor—jewelry—and a robe!

(Moves closer)

Impossible! No, really—! What? I've read
Willpower can move mountains round the globe,
But can it also move a thoroughbred?
Who cares? The fact is here's a horse to go on.
Ab esse ad posse, et cetera and so on.

(Puts the robe on and looks down)

Sir Peter, and a Turk from head to toe!
I'll say one thing—oh, boy, you never know!

(Climbs into the saddle)

Giddyup, Dobbin! Come on, horse, let's go!
A golden stirrup—hey! They say you know
A man by how he sits his horse? Just so!

(He gallops into the desert)

A tent of an Arab sheik at an oasis. Peer Gynt, in his eastern robe, reclines on some cushions. He's drinking coffee and smoking a long pipe. Anitra, with a group of other girls, dances and sings for him.

GIRLS' CHOIR:
   The prophet has come!
   The prophet, the one who will understand,
   To us, to us he has come
   Riding the ocean of sand!
   The prophet, the one who will light up our land,
   To us, to us he has come

Sailing the ocean of sand!
Play on the flute and the drum;
The prophet, the prophet has come!

ANITRA:

His horse is white, the milky white
Which flows in the streams of Paradise.
Lower your heads! Seek his advice!
His eyes are stars, twinkling and bright.
Those stars have rays which give off rays
At which no child of the earth may gaze.
Into the desert he has come.
Gold chains and pearls he has strewn about.
Where he is riding, there is light.
Behind him there was only night;
Behind him was simoom and drought.
He, the almighty one, has come!
Into the desert he has come
Dressed as a son of the earth!
The kaaba, the kaaba is empty and dumb,
And he will give us rebirth!

GIRLS' CHOIR:

Play on the flute and the drum
The prophet, the prophet has come!

(The music is muted; the girls go on dancing)

PEER GYNT:

I read somewhere—and now I understand—
"No one can be a prophet in his own land."
This is a much more palatable life
Than Charlestown, with the worry and the strife
Of business! All that had a hollow ring;
Beneath was something strange and worrying;

It made me ill at ease—I'll make a small confession—
The company I kept—as well as the profession.
And why was I involved in all those highjinks?
Why was I messing in the business world?
Now when I try to understand, my heart sinks;
I guess it's just the way the planets twirled.
To be yourself only because you're rich—
You might as well build houses on the sand;
For watches, rings and other contraband,
Men wag their tails and wallow in a ditch!
They lift their hats if they should see a big cigar!
But money doesn't tell what kind of man you are!
To be a prophet, though, is thrilling;
You know just where you stand, what you achieve;
If you're successful, you *yourself* receive
The credit, not the pound and shilling.
You're what you are without a lot of froufrou;
You also aren't forever saying thank you
And plotting how to make another killing.
Prophet! It's something I can understand!
It happened rather unexpectedly—
Crossing the desert unsuspectingly,
I chanced to meet these children of the sand.
The prophet had arrived! They were frenetic!
It wasn't my intention to deceive them—
A lie is not the same as a prophetic
Response! Moreover, I can always leave them;
I'm not tied down! It's an ideal scenario:
For once there won't be any hitch or complication!
My horse is saddled up—nearby—ready to go—
In short, I am the master of the situation.

ANITRA *(Approaching the entrance)*:
    Prophet and master!

PEER GYNT:

What is wrong, my dear?

ANITRA:

Sons of the desert wait before your tent.
They want to see your face—

PEER GYNT:

Tell them to stay!
Tell them that they must all stay far away.
Tell them that I can hear each one's lament.
Tell them I tolerate no men in here!
My child, men have a lousy pedigree—
They have less spine than an invertebrate!
You can't imagine, child, how shamelessly
They've swind—or sinned is more appropriate.
Well, that's that! Ladies, dance for me!
Erase this vexing memory!

GIRLS *(Dancing)*:

The prophet is good! The prophet is sad
Because the sons of the sand have been bad!
The prophet is merciful—mercy be blest!
He has opened Paradise for the oppressed!

PEER GYNT *(Eyes following Anitra during the dance)*:

Her legs move faster than a drummer's sticks.
I'll bet that piece of baggage knows some tricks!
Her shape's a bit extravagant;
Her beauty isn't elegant
But what is beauty but a style,
A coin, usable for a while.
The norm deprives us of the real treasure—
Extravagance is what will give us pleasure!
I want too much, or else I want too little;
I'm sick of everything that's in the middle.
Both young and old arouse my lust—

The in-between earns my disgust.
Her feet have not been washed too thoroughly,
Nor have her arms—they're a bit garlicky.
But *that*, you see, will cause me no malaise;
I'd rather say I'm going through a phase—
Anitra, listen!

ANITRA *(Approaching him)*:

      Yes? Your slave has heard.

PEER GYNT:

You are bewitching, child. The prophet is stirred.
You don't believe me? Here's the proof, my little plum—
I will make you a houri in the life to come!

ANITRA:

Master, that cannot be!

PEER GYNT:

            You think I'm lying?
I swear it's true—I'm not just speechifying!

ANITRA:

But I have no soul.

PEER GYNT:

          Then thou shallst havest one!

ANITRA:

How, my lord?

PEER GYNT:

        Don't you worry how it's done!
I will take care of it—don't fret!
No soul? Yes, as they say, dumb as a post.
I've noted it with some regret.
But for a soul there's always room—almost
Always, at least. Come, let me have a look—
There's room! I *knew* that I was not mistook!
To tell the truth, you won't have an outstanding
Or *large* soul—that's a little too demanding—

But what the hell—who cares? That's all the same!
You'll have enough; there won't be any shame!

ANITRA:

The prophet is good . . .

PEER GYNT:

You're hesitating, girl?

ANITRA:

I'd rather have . . .

PEER GYNT:

Speak up! Don't hesitate!

ANITRA:

A soul's not much; it's really not so great;
But if you'd give me . . .

PEER GYNT:

What?

ANITRA *(Pointing at his turban)*:

. . . yon gorgeous pearl!

PEER GYNT *(Enraptured, he hands her the jewel)*:

Anitra! Oh, in Eve's own image you are bred!
Like metal to a magnet is the pull upon
This man! For as some writer or another said—
I'm quoting now—"*das ewig weibliche zieht uns an!*"[20]

Moonlight. A palm grove outside Anitra's tent. Peer Gynt sits under a tree, a lute in hand. His beard and hair have been trimmed; he looks substantially younger.

PEER GYNT *(Plays and sings)*:
    I lock the door of Paradise
    And throw away the key.

I cross the ocean in a trice,
While ladies wail their sacrifice
Upon the northern lee.

We make sail south, then farther south,
On winds that never tire.
Where palms sway in the land of drouth—
A moustache on the ocean's mouth—
I set my ship on fire.

I climb on board the ship of the sand,
The ship that has four legs.
It foams when stung by my whip hand.
I am a giddy songbird, and
A bird who trills and begs!

Anitra, nectar of the palm!
I'm telling truly now!
Angoran goat cheese cannot calm
My appetite with half the balm
Anitra, dear, as thou!

(Shifts the lute over his shoulder and approaches)

Hush! Does my little beauty listen?
Has my love sung along?
Behind the curtain does she glisten,
Undressing to my song?
What's that? A cork? Is my adoring
One opening a bottle?
It's lechery at full throttle!
Again! It's something glottal—
Ah, it's Anitra—and she's snoring!
Sweet tones! Anitra's sleeping.

Nightingale, stop! It's impolite!
You and I soon will have a fight
If you keep up that weeping!
But—as it's written—who cares! Right?
The nightingale's a singer,
And I'm a singer, too, tonight.
He and I both captivate hearts
By plying all our musical arts.
The still of night is made for scales;
Song is our guiding star—
We sing, therefore we are
Us, Peer Gynt and the nightingales!
The lady sleeps? She's doing me a favor—
She prolongs my amorous delight,
Permitting me to hold the dish and savor
The aroma prior to a bite—
Oh, she's awake! That's a close call!
I guess that's better, after all.

ANITRA *(From the tent)*:

Master, you called? It's late! Was that
Your voice?

PEER GYNT:

The prophet called! And how!
I was awakened by a cat
Prowling around. It howled just now—

ANITRA:

Master, that cat was not just prowling;
Some other movement caused that yowling.

PEER GYNT:

What was it?

ANITRA:

Oh, have mercy!

PEER GYNT:
                    Girl,

    Speak!
ANITRA:
                    Oh, I'm blushing—
PEER GYNT *(Closer)*:
                              Was it, perhaps,
    The kind of passion that enwraps
    My soul when I give you a pearl?
ANITRA *(Distressed)*:
    I can't make a comparison like that!
    The treasured prophet to a mangy cat!
PEER GYNT:
    Child, from an amorous point of view,
    Prophets and tomcats—*entre nous*—
    Have similar ends that they pursue.
ANITRA:
    Master, your sense of humor always grabs
    Me where I am most vulnerable!
PEER GYNT:
                    My dear,
    You—just like all of womankind—appear
    To judge a man by nothing but his scabs.
    Deep down, my pet, I'm full of fun,
    Particularly face to face.
    But one's position urges one
    To soberly maintain one's place.
    My hands are tied by obligation,
    The judgments in each person's case
    —I take such pains with big and small—
    Make a prophetical grimace
    From all the heavy concentration.

Not now, though! In a tête-à-tête
I'm Peer—the Peerest of them all!
The prophet we will now forget
And Peer himself is in your thrall!

(Sits down under a tree and pulls her to him)

Anitra, let us rest a while
Under the fan of the green palm!
And while I whisper, you will smile;
And then will come your turn, madame,
Your lusty lips will whisper love
While I smile! Little turtle-dove!

ANITRA *(Lies down at his feet)*:

Each word is sweeter than a song
Although I really do not understand.
Master, were you to issue the command,
Could I acquire a soul?

PEER GYNT:

It's wrong
To talk about the soul right now.
We'll do it later on, I vow.
When in the east the rosy rays
Of gold proclaim that day is here,
Then, my girl, I will try to raise
Your consciousness to higher spheres.
But in the heat and still of night,
It is stupidity or spite
To play the role of pedagogue
With some decrepit monologue!
The soul, quite frankly, dear, amounts
To nothing in our earthly phase.
The heart—the heart!—is all that counts!

ANITRA:

    Oh, master, speak to your slave girl!
    Each word is like a shining pearl!

PEER GYNT:

    Too much wit is stupidity;
    Faintheartedness, iniquity.
    And truthfulness exaggerated
    Is wisdom that is mutilated.
    And, my child, beat me like a dog
    If it's not true—those whose whole
    Lives are devoted to the soul
    Are doomed to wander in a fog.
    I knew somebody like that once,
    A gem of flawless eminence;
    But even he lost sight of what his goal
    Was, deafened by the silence of the soul.
    Look 'round at this desert domain.
    All I need do is lift my turban
    And oceans from Stockholm to Durban
    Would come rushing in to flood the plain.
    But what a dodo I would be
    To change the world's geography!
    Do you know what it means to live?

ANITRA:

    Tell!

PEER GYNT:

        To glide down the primitive
    River of time, never forgetting
    To be yourself, and never letting
    Your feet get wet! The currency
    Of self, my dear, is potency!
    Old eagles molt and lose their feathers,
    Old cobblers start to stoop, old wethers

Bleat, and old biddies lose their teeth,
Old men can't stay dry underneath,
And each one has a shriveled soul.
I want to rule as sultans rule—
Impassioned, young, out of control!
Not on the banks of Gyntiana
Or over palm trees and savanna—
But in the tender vestibule
Of some young virginal Diana.
Now, my girl, do you fathom me?
That I might be your Bonaparte,
That I might captivate your heart—
That's the foundation, don't you see,
On which I'll build my caliphate
Of self! I'll own your every desire!
Physical force rules in the state
Of Gyntian love! You're mine and mine alone!
My manliness demands that I acquire
You like a golden coin or precious stone.
If we should part, then life is over—
At least, for *you*! So note it well, my own!
Every inch of you, moreover,
Must be devoid of will—of yes
And no—and filled with my *noblesse*.
Your beauty, your nocturnal gift—
Everything that I gaze upon—
Has set my sultan's heart adrift,
Transporting me to Babylon.
And come to think of it, it's good
That you have no imagination.
Had you one, in all likelihood
You'd give yourself consideration.
Listen, my little honey bee,

Wouldn't a golden anklet show
How much I care? Or two? Or three?
As for a soul, don't worry so,
My dear. Let's just reserve that space for me,
And for the rest—it's *status quo*.

(*Anitra snores*)

What? Is she sleeping? Has my flower
Not heard what I was saying? Could it be?
No! It just demonstrates the power
Of my impassioned exposé!
It's made her swoon, swept her away!

(*Gets up and puts jewelry in her lap*)

Take these! There will be more, I swear!
Sleep now, Anitra! Dream of Peer—
Sleep! In your sleep you place the crown
Upon your loving Peer's imperial brow!
This is my moment of renown;
Anitra wished to sleep—I showed her how!

A caravan route. The oasis far behind in the distance. Peer Gynt, on his white horse, gallops across the desert. Anitra is in front of him, on the pommel.

ANITRA:
    Stop or I'll bite you!
PEER GYNT:
                    Sweetie pie, let's talk!
ANITRA:
    What do you want?

PEER GYNT:

You're the sparrow—I'm the hawk!
I want to play wild games! Let's play abduction!

ANITRA:

Shame! An old prophet—

PEER GYNT:

Fiddle-de-dee!
The prophet isn't old! You see?
Are old men capable of reproduction?

ANITRA:

Take me home! Stop it! Filthy brute!

PEER GYNT:

Home, eh? Go home to daddy? Oh, how cute!
Once a mad bird has flown its cage,
He'll not endure an in-law's rage
A second time, my child. And anyway,
If you've been in one place too long, why stay?
You gain acquaintances but not appreciation—
For prophets, these words are especially true—
Here and gone, like a song you've listened to
Once. I would say it's time to end this visitation.
Sons of the desert, child, are fickle fare;
I left, and there was no incense or prayer!

ANITRA:

Are you a prophet?

PEER GYNT:

No! Emperor!

(Tries to kiss her)

And
Look how the woodpecker makes a stubborn stand!

ANITRA:

Why not be nice? Give me that ring.

PEER GYNT:

Take it, Anitra—it's a little trinket!

ANITRA:

Your words are songs that make hearts sing!

PEER GYNT:

That I am loved so dearly! Who would think it!
I'll lead the horse! I want to be your slave!

(Hands her the whip and gets down)

My little flower! Little rose! Observe
How I will struggle through the sand and brave
A sunstroke just to get what I deserve!
I'm young, Anitra! Don't you see?
So judge my stunts accordingly.
Mischief and pranks are marks of youth!
And if you'd only be a little less contrary,
My blossom, you'd perceive the truth—
I'm full of pranks—ergo, I'm young!

ANITRA:

                    Extraordinary!
Yes, you are young! Have you another ring?

PEER GYNT:

I'm a young buck! Yes! Take the dirty thing!
I'd wear a wreath of vine leaves, given half a chance!
Yes, by God, I am young! And now I want to dance!

(Dances and sings)

        I am a lucky rooster!
        Give me a peck, my little hen!
        Hey, watch me kick! Hey, watch me spin!
        I am a lucky rooster!

ANITRA:

Prophet, you're sweating—I'm afraid you'll melt!
Give me that thing that's dangling from your belt.

PEER GYNT:

> Such tender loving care! Here, take the purse—
> We lovers need no gold; it's just a curse!

(Dances and sings again)

> Peer Gynt is such a wild young man!
> He doesn't know where he will fall.
> Who cares, says Peer—who cares at all!
> Peer Gynt is such a wild young man!

ANITRA:

> How comely is the prophet's dance!

PEER GYNT:

> To hell with prophets—now's your chance
> To wear prophetic clothes! Take them off!

ANITRA:

> No!
>
> They wouldn't fit! It's just not apropos!

PEER GYNT:

> *Eh bien*!

(Kneels)

> But please give me a heartache
> For lovers need the pain of heartbreak!
> We'll enter through my castle gates some day—

ANITRA:

> In Paradise! Do we have far to ride?

PEER GYNT:

> Oh, several thousand miles—

ANITRA:

> Too far!

PEER GYNT:

> But I'd
> Look for the soul I promised on the way—

ANITRA:

    I'll get along without a soul, thank you.

    But didn't you just ask me for a little pain?

PEER GYNT:

    Damn, yes! Poignant, but quick—one day would do!

ANITRA:

    Anitra must obey the Prophet—*auf wiedersehen*!

    (She gives him a good thwack on the fingers, and heads back into the desert at a gallop)

PEER GYNT *(Transfixed for a long time, as if struck by lightning)*:
    Well, I'll be . . . !

Same place. One hour later. Peer Gynt, calmly and reflectively, removes the Turkish clothing piece by piece. Finally, he takes a cap out of his coat pocket, puts it on, and is once more in European dress.

PEER GYNT *(Throwing the turban away)*:
    There lies the Turk, and here am I!
    I swear I'll never prophesy
    Again. Lucky it's clothing—that's what I think—;
    Not, as they say, a cut in the eye!
    How did I get involved in all those highjinks?
    It's best to lead a Christian way of life,
    To be untouched by pride and vanity,
    A pillar of old-time morality,
    True to yourself, ending your earthly strife
    With a few words of generality
    Beside the grave.

    (Walks a few steps)

That baggage came an eyelash
Away from making my head turn.
Why did I let her pull me by my moustache?
Damned if I'm able to discern
Her great appeal! I'm just incredulous!
She almost made me look ridiculous!
I was mistaken. It's a consolation
That it was all due to the situation—
It wasn't really me! To be precise,
It's thanks to all this prophet brouhaha
That's altogether lacking in the spice
Of life, and so induces nausea—
And poor taste. Yes, this prophet business keeps you
                        humble!
In your professional capacity
You must pretend you're in a fog; what makes you stumble
Is rashly showing the audacity
To act like you're awake! That was the only
Reason I ever flirted with that lonely
Thing in the first place.

(Breaks out laughing)

I can dream, can't I?
Of stopping time with a few spins and dips,
Fighting the flow with movement of the hips!
To play a lute, to pitch a little woo—
And get plucked like a hen—it happened, boy, to you!
That must be what it means to prophesy.
Plucked! Damn, I'd say so! Did she ever pluck
Me clean. I had the foresight—or the luck—
To hold on to what little money's in my pants,
And in America there's more—I have a chance!
From here on in, I'll walk the middle road—it's best

Not to be weighted down by gold, or overdressed—
In short, just as they say in some translation,
I'll be the master of the situation.
First, choose your path! Many are beckoning;
The choice will tell—by most men's reckoning—
The wise man from the fool. Well, business is
A book that's closed. My love life lost its fizz.
No going backward now! For it is said,
"It's just as far, forward or back;
Outside or in looks just as black,"
It's in some book or other that I've read.
So something new! Something uplifting, too;
A goal that's worthy of my derring-do.
Perhaps I'll write my own biography
To give men hope—a hagiography
That—wait! I have the time! I could apply
Myself to studying greed in times gone by!
I've the *curriculum vitae*, don't I?
Yes, *this* is really something I should do!
I read a lot of history as a little child,
My mind's unprejudiced—it's almost undefiled!
I'll be the one who gives mankind its due!
Feather-like, I will float on history's stream,
Living it all again as in a dream,
See heroes battle for the greater good—
At a safe distance, be it understood—
See wise men rise and fall, see martyrs bleed,
See the colossal empires come and go,
See epochs taking shape in embryo!
I'll skim the tide of history! I'll need
An almanac or something in my hand
To check on dates and help me understand
The world's events. My learning's not too thorough,

And so details I'll have to steal or borrow—
Who cares—a point of view that's marginal
Is sure to be the most original.
It is ennobling to set one's keel
To reach one's goal—but it takes nerves of steel!

(Hushed and emotional)

To break forever all the ties that bind
Us to our native soil and our own kind,
To blow to pieces every earthly good,
To bid farewell to love and womanhood—
And all for what? To solve the mystery
Of life!

(Wipes a tear from his eye)

        Well, isn't *that* what history
Is all about? I feel such great felicity!
At last I've solved the riddle of my destiny.
All I must do—no matter what—through thick and thin—
Is persevere! And if I stand erect
And say that I'm Peer Gynt, or (more correct)
The Emperor of History—that's no sin!
I want to own the answers to the past;
The present time is much too crude—roughcast.
I'd like to spare you all the sordid detail
But!—Modern man's a hypocrite and petty—
Hearts without wings, deeds without weight—

(Shrugs his shoulders)

        and yet he
Is a damn sight better than your modern female!

(He leaves)

Summer day. A mountain cabin in the north, deep in the forest. A door with a big wooden bolt, open. Reindeer antlers over the door. A herd of goats beside the cabin. A radiantly attractive middle-aged woman sits outside—in a sunny spot—spinning.

WOMAN *(Glancing down the path and singing)*:
Winter and spring will disappear; they'll disappear.
Even summer, even a year, will disappear.
But one day you'll return to me; you'll come, I know;
Until that day, I'll wait for you; I'll wait as I promised long
ago.

(Calls the goats, then spins and sings again)

God give you strength if you are all alone; if you are all alone!
God bless you if you stand before his throne—oh, kneel
before his throne!
Here I will await your return, my love—until you come,
my friend.
And if you're with God, I will come to you; I promise
I'll join you in the end.[21]

In Egypt. Daybreak. The Memnon[22] statue in the sand. Peer Gynt walks up to it and looks around.

PEER GYNT:
A fine place to begin the first inscriptions
Of my research. Today, we are Egyptians;
Egyptian but still Gyntian.
Next we will be Assyrian.
To start with the creation of the world

Would just get all my whys and wherefores swirled,
So I think I'll sidestep the Bible.
(For after all, it's just a tribal
History.) I don't need to scrutinize
Things with a microscope, you realize.

(Sits down on a rock)

Now I will rest and wait with great intensity
Till this old man shows his renowned propensity
For singing. Then I'll climb the pyramid,
And if I can, I'll see what all is hid
Inside. The great historiographer
Will then discover where King Potiphar
Is buried. Later, I'll become an Asian fellow,
Who finds the famous hanging garden and bordello—
High water marks, you must admit—of Babylon.
Next, in one jump, the wall of Troy. I'll travel on
From Troy, cross the Aegean Sea to Greece,
To Athens! Home of Lysias and Phidias!
Then—on the scene—in professorial peace
And quiet, I'll inspect the pass Leonidas
Defended, get acquainted with philosophy,
And there where Socrates met his catastrophe
I'll pause and—wait! The Greeks are in a war!
You'd think they would have stopped all that before
I made my travel plans!

(Looks at his watch)

                    Why does it take
So long to see a sunrise? Time is short!
I'd best go back to Troy—that was the port—

(Stands up and listens)

What's that peculiar sound, for heaven's sake?

(Sunrise)

THE MEMNON STATUE *(Singing)*:
> The birds of rejuvenation
> Are singing in jubilation
> In the ashes of the demigod.
> For Zeus, at their creation
> Set them in disputation.
> Owl of wisdom, tell
> Where do my birds dwell?
> Solve the riddle of the song!
> You will die if you are wrong!

PEER GYNT:
> That sounded like the statue! Yes, at last
> It sang—I heard it! Music of the past!
> I heard its voice! The harmony of stone!
> I think I'll write this down and make it known
> Among my colleagues!

(Writing in his notebook)

> "Heard the statue sing,
> Although I didn't understand a thing.
> Just an hallucination, I would say.
> Nothing important, then, observed today."

(Walks off)

The village of Giza. The Great Stone Sphinx. In the distance, the minarets and spires of Cairo. Peer Gynt comes in; he looks at the Sphinx carefully, first through a pince-nez, then through his cupped hand.

PEER GYNT:

> This monstrous thing, for heaven's sake, calls forth
> Some distant memory from who knows where.
> Once something like it crossed my path—up north?
> Was it a person? If so, who? I swear—
> Now that I think on it—the Memnon statue
> Resembled the Old Man of Dovre, in the way
> He sat there, stiff with some arthritic ague,
> His rear end planted on a primitive array
> Of broken columns. This strange mongrel, though—
> Part lion and part woman potpourri—
> From fairy tales, perhaps? Or do I know
> That face because it jogs my memory?
> From fairy tales! No, I remember now!
> God! It's the Great Between! Remember how
> I beat him up?—I think—I had a fever
> Then!

(Goes closer)

> The same mouth, same eyes—a true deceiver!
> More cunning than before, not quite so tame,
> But otherwise, he's just about the same. ·
> So, Between, when one sees you in the day
> You are a lion, eh, from a posterior view!
> You still like riddles? What have you to say?
> Let's just see if you answer like you used to do!

(Shouts at the Sphinx)

> Hey, who are you, Between?

VOICE:

> *Ach, wer bist du,*
> Sphinx?

PEER GYNT:

> What was that? A German echo? Odd!

VOICE:

> *Wer bist du?*

PEER GYNT:

> A fluent German echo! God!
> This observation's new—and mine!

(Writes in his notebook)

> Wherein
> "Echo in German. Dialect—Berlin."

(Begriffenfeldt[23] emerges from behind the Sphinx)

BEGRIFFENFELDT:

> A man!

PEER GYNT:

> Oh, *that's* what's causing the confusion.

(Makes more notes)

> "Later arrived at different conclusion."

BEGRIFFENFELDT *(With all kinds of nervous gestures)*:

> Oh, please excuse me, sir! A *Lebensfrage*[24]!
> What has made you come here today?

PEER GYNT:

> A visit to a friend, I'd say.

BEGRIFFENFELDT:

> The Sphinx?

PEER GYNT *(Nods)*:

> A hero in my personal saga.

BEGRIFFENFELDT:

> Of course! And coming after such a night!
> My head is throbbing—ready to explode!
> What is he? Answer me! Might you decode
> His secret? Speak!

PEER GYNT:

> His secret? Yes, I might!
> He is *himself.*

BEGRIFFENFELDT *(With a start)*:

A flash of lightning in the sky
Answers the mystery of life! You're positive
He is himself?

PEER GYNT:

On that he's been definitive.

BEGRIFFENFELDT:

Himself! The hour of revolution now is nigh!

(Takes off his hat)

Your name, sir?

PEER GYNT:

I was baptized as Peer Gynt.

BEGRIFFENFELDT *(In quiet admiration)*:

Peer Gynt! Allegorical! Just as I expected!
Peer Gynt? The unknown one—the one who is elected
Has come! I was, of course, given a hint—

PEER GYNT:

You're here to meet—? My God, I wouldn't have
suspected—

BEGRIFFENFELDT:

Peer Gynt! Deep! Full of riddles! Yes, a book
Which must be read—each word a mystery!
What are you?

PEER GYNT *(Modestly)*:

I have always tried to be
Myself. Here is my passport—take a look!

BEGRIFFENFELDT:

The mystery of life!

(Grabbing his wrist)

To Cairo! I have found
The emperor of enlightenment! He must be crowned!

PEER GYNT:
>   Emperor?
BEGRIFFENFELDT:
>   Come!
PEER GYNT:
>   It's quite a compliment—
BEGRIFFENFELDT *(Pulling him along)*:
>   All hail the emperor of enlightenment!
>   Self is his true and only fundament!

In Cairo. A large courtyard surrounded by high walls and build-ings. Barred windows; metal cages. Three guards in the yard. A fourth comes in.

THE ONE ARRIVING:
>   Hey, Schafman! Where's the doctor? Where'd he go?
GUARD:
>   He left before the sunrise—long before.
FIRST:
>   Not good! Something went wrong last night, you know,
>   And I think—
ANOTHER:
>   Quiet, shh! He's at the door!

(Begriffenfeldt ushers Peer Gynt in, locks the gate and puts the key in his pocket)

PEER GYNT *(To himself)*:
>   The man's extraordinarily well-read;
>   I haven't understood a word he's said.

(Looking around)

This is the lodge of learned men?

BEGRIFFENFELDT:

Here you will find them! All of them are here—
The circle of three score and ten[25]—
Grown by one hundred sixty just this year!

(Shouts at the guards)

Mikkel and Schlingenberg, Schafman and Fox[26]—
Into your cages—now!—and lock the locks!

GUARDS:

Me? Us?

BEGRIFFENFELDT:

          Who else? Get moving—in with you!
When the world turns over, we turn over, too!

(He pushes them into a cage)

He came to us this morning—Peer the Great—
And thou shalt join the others—no debate!

(Locks the cage and throws the key down the well)

PEER GYNT:

But my dear Doctor! Dear Director—please!

BEGRIFFENFELDT:

That's long ago! Now I am none of these!
Aaah! Can you keep a secret, Mr. Peer?

PEER GYNT:

What?

BEGRIFFENFELDT:

        But you must not let this traumatize
You, man!

PEER GYNT:

            I'll try—

BEGRIFFENFELDT *(Pulls him into a corner and whispers)*:

        This very night—prepare

Yourself now!—common sense met its demise!

PEER GYNT:

    My God!

BEGRIFFENFELDT:

              Yes, isn't it regrettable?
For me, it's doubly unforgettable
Because this was—until the revolution—
A mental institution.

PEER GYNT:

                Institution!

BEGRIFFENFELDT:

    Not *now*, you understand!

PEER GYNT *(Pale, in a low voice)*:

               Yes, now I see!
The man is mad—and no one knows but me!

(Pulls away)

BEGRIFFENFELDT *(Follows him)*:

    You follow me, sir? Can you take this in?
I say he's dead—but it's a paradox.
He's taken leave of himself, and of his skin,
Just like—you know—Baron Munchhausen's fox.[27]

PEER GYNT:

    Excuse me, please—

BEGRIFFENFELDT *(Holding on to him)*:

            Or no—more like an eel,
Not like a fox. A needle through the eye—
He squirms against the wall—

PEER GYNT:

             Sir, I appeal—

BEGRIFFENFELDT:

    One cut around the throat, then skin—goodbye!

PEER GYNT:

    He's mad! Out of his senses totally!

BEGRIFFENFELDT:

    Now it is clear—never again obscure—
    To take leave of oneself is to assure
    A revolution both on land and sea.
    All those who used to be insane
    Are cured as of tonight! The reign
    Of common sense has entered a new phase!
    It's also certain (viewed from this, the right
    Perspective)—as of ten o'clock tonight—
    The so-called wise men now are in a daze.

PEER GYNT:

    You mentioned time; mine, I'm afraid, is short—

BEGRIFFENFELDT:

    Your time? Exactly the correct retort!

(Opens the door and shouts)

    Out! See the future! Common sense is dead!
    Long live Peer Gynt, who now will rule instead!

PEER GYNT:

    But—

(The inmates slowly come into the yard)

BEGRIFFENFELDT:

        The dawn of liberation lights the sky!
    Can we not say good morning? Let us try!
    Your emperor has come!

PEER GYNT:

            Emperor?

BEGRIFFENFELDT:

                Yes!

PEER GYNT:

    The honor is too great—it couldn't be—

BEGRIFFENFELDT:

    Oh, please! Let us have no false modesty—
    Not at a time like this!

PEER GYNT:

                  Oh, what a mess!
    Really, I'm speechless! I'm not good enough!

BEGRIFFENFELDT:

    A man who is himself? Who has the stuff
    To solve the mystery of the Sphinx?

PEER GYNT:

                 But I'd
    Say that's the problem! I'm myself—it's true!
    But in this situation, I would do
    Much better if I were—you know!—beside
    Myself!

BEGRIFFENFELDT:

          Beside yourself? Totally wrong!
    In here, you're nothing but yourself from A
    To Z. Your naked self is on display.
    The self, under full sail, barrels along.
    Each one has closed himself up in the keg
    Of self; each one's lost in self-fermentation.
    The bung of self is closed—the isolation
    Is total, sealing in a pickled dreg
    Of self. No one will listen to someone explain;
    No one will sympathize with someone else's pain.
    We are ourselves—in thought, in word, and deed;
    Poised at the very edge—ourselves through and through!
    So if an emperor is what we need,
    It's clear that it should be no one but you.

PEER GYNT:

Oh, God, get—

BEGRIFFENFELDT:

Please! A little discipline!
In the beginning, everything is new!
Come! I'll show you a perfect specimen
Of "selfness." I will choose at random—you!

(To a shadowy figure)

Huhu! Hello! Here's someone you should get
To know. Why are you always so upset?

HUHU:

Why not? My ancestors are dead
Without being interpreted!

(To Peer Gynt)

A stranger! Do you want to hear?

PEER GYNT *(Bows)*:

By all means!

HUHU:

Good! Lend me your ear!
Wreathing the land of India—far
Away—is the beach of Malabar.
The Portuguese and German nations
Have introduced their civilizations,
And, of course, you know that there are
The genuine natives of Malabar.
Man's sovereignty is undeterred;
My language has been massacred.
But long ago, you are aware,
Orangutans were masters there,
Lords of the jungle. They could growl
Or grab, and they could fight and howl
The way that nature had intended;

They cried and screamed, and they depended
On no one else to tell them how!
They were the royalty! But now
These foreign devils are among
Us and pollute our primal tongue!
A night of several hundred thousand years
Eclipses both the monkey and his peers.
Anyone knows a night that long
Kills everyone—the weak and strong.
The jungle's lost its primal roar;
There is no growling anymore.
The only easel for our thoughts
Holds words and speech, but that cannot
Suffice! And all have the disease—
The Germans and the Portuguese,
The Malabarians and the half-breeds—
For each and every one my heart bleeds.
I struggled long to cultivate
Our language—reinvigorate
The corpse—and thus reclaim the jungle dream
Of the inalienable right to scream.
I scream myself, and I have long
Endorsed and cheered its use in song,
But few, I fear, share my belief.
And now you understand my grief.
Thank you for having lent your ear;
Have you advice? Please let me hear!

PEER GYNT *(In a low voice)*:

It has been said that if you prowl
With wolves, you'd better learn to howl.

(Out loud)

My dearest friend, there's an atoll

In the Pacific, I recall,
Where an orangutan can get along
Without the use of speech or even song;
Their speech is Malabarian—
It's primal and barbarian—
Can't you—and all like-minded men—
Emigrate and begin again—?

HUHU:

Thank you for having lent your ear;
Because of you, my path is clear.

(With a grand gesture)

The western world wants only flunkies!
The Orient is ruled by monkeys!

(He leaves)

BEGRIFFENFELDT:

Was he *himself*? I think he's shown
He's true to self—*himself* alone!
He radiates *himself*! He doesn't hide
Himself, not even when he is beside
Himself. Come here! Here is one—don't be frightened—
Who, since this evening, is no less enlightened.

(To a Fellah, who is carrying a mummy on his back)

King Apis! How is everything, your highness?

FELLAH *(To Peer Gynt, maniacally)*:

Am I King Apis?

PEER GYNT *(Hiding behind the Doctor)*:

Please forgive my shyness,
But I'm not really qualified to say—
Although you have a certain *je ne sais*—

FELLAH:

You're lying, too!

BEGRIFFENFELDT:

Would you not fill

Us in, your highness?

FELLAH:

That I will.

(Turns to Peer Gynt)

Do you see who I carry on my back?
King Apis used to be his name,
But now he's going by the name of mummy—
He's dead, no matter what his fame.
He built the pyramids—
Oh, yes!—he carved the great stone Sphinx,
And fought—the Doctor says—
Against the Turk, both *rechts* and *links*.[28]
And therefore all of Egypt
Prays to King Apis now,
Placing him in their temples
Just like a sacred cow.
But *I* am this King Apis!
That I can clearly see;
If you don't understand it
My friend, listen to me.
King Apis was out hunting
And needed some relief.
He used the bushes on
My father's land. In brief,
The field he fertilized
Has fed *me* with its corn!
You think that it's untrue?
Look! An invisible horn!
And isn't it just hell

That no one prays to me?
By birthright I'm King Apis,
But a peasant's all they see!
    Please tell me what to do—
Don't lie! Or hesitate!
How do I claim my rights
As king—Apis the Great!

PEER GYNT:

    Your highness must build pyramids—
Oh, yes!—and carve a larger Sphinx,
And fight—just as the Doctor says—
Against the Turk, both *rechts* and *links*.

FELLAH:

    Oh, what a pretty speech!
I am a fellah! I'm a louse!
I cannot even keep
The rats out of my house!
    Now think of something better,
Man, take another tack!
Something so I'll be like
The king who's on my back!

PEER GYNT:

    What if your highness hanged himself?
And then nothing more need be said,
For in the coffin, underground,
You could pretend that you were dead!

FELLAH:

    My kingdom for a rope!
What an idea! Truly sublime!
At first it may seem odd,
But all will be the same with time.

(Goes to the side and makes preparations as if to hang himself)

BEGRIFFENFELDT:

He's really quite a fellow, isn't he?

A man of method, Mister Peer—

PEER GYNT:

I see—

He did it! Hanged himself! No! The poor soul!

I'm going to be sick—I've lost control!

BEGRIFFENFELDT:

It's only a transition; it will pass.

PEER GYNT:

I'm leaving—what! Transition, eh? My ass!

BEGRIFFENFELDT *(Holding him back)*:

Are you mad?

PEER GYNT:

Mad? Not yet! Take those flea-bitten—

(Commotion. His Excellency Hussein forces his way through the crowd)

HUSSEIN:

I'm told an emperor arrived today.

(To Peer Gynt)

That's you?

PEER GYNT *(In despair)*:

It's me. At least, that's what they say.

HUSSEIN:

You have communiques that must be written?

PEER GYNT *(Pulling his hair)*:

Oh, sure! Why not? The worse it gets, the better!

HUSSEIN:

Perhaps I could help you to write a letter?

(A deep bow)

I am a pen.

PEER GYNT *(An even deeper bow)*:
> I'm the imaginary
> Scrawl on a royal piece of stationery.

HUSSEIN:
> My history is brief; I'll say it once again!
> I cannot be a blotter, sir—I am a pen!

PEER GYNT:
> My history, sir, is even shorter—I'll be frank,
> I am a piece of paper destined to be blank.

HUSSEIN:
> People don't understand what I'm about—
> All they would like to do is dry me out!

PEER GYNT:
> I was a book with gilded edges, owned by a girl—
> Whether you're mad or sane—a grain of sand or a pearl—
> It's nothing but a typographical mistake!

HUSSEIN:
> Dip me in ink! I am a pen, for heaven's sake!

PEER GYNT *(Leaping around)*:
> Please let me be a buck, leaping up high
> Above the ground, flying across the sky!

HUSSEIN:
> A knife! I'm dull! Someone must scrape and sharpen me!
> The earth will split if I'm not sharpened instantly!

PEER GYNT:
> The Lord looked at the world that he himself had made
> By hand and said—of course—"Well done!" What a
> > charade!

BEGRIFFENFELDT:
> Here is a knife!

HUSSEIN *(Grabbing it)*:
> > Watch how the ink flows from the gash!
> Oh, what a joy to cut oneself!

(Cuts his throat)

BEGRIFFENFELDT *(Stepping aside)*:
                    Watch out! Don't splash!
PEER GYNT *(In great torment)*:
    Hold him!
HUSSEIN:
            Yes, hold me! If you think that you are able!
    Hold the pen! Hold me! Toward the paper on the table—!

(Falls)

    I'm tired. Please don't forget to write my postscript, friend:
    "He lived and died a pen—a pen until the end!"
PEER GYNT *(About to faint)*:
    What should I—! What am I—! No, don't—wait, wait!
    I'll be just what you want—! I'll follow all the rules!
    A sinner, Turk or troll—You who create—

(Screams)

    I can't remember—what's your name! Wait! Wait!
    Oh, you know who you are—! Protector of the fools!

(Collapses, exhausted)

BEGRIFFENFELDT *(Jumps on top of him and sits, holding a wreath of straw)*:
    Beside himself! Out with the old and ring
    In the new! He's the one, true heir
    To the throne of self! Hooray!

(Places the wreath on his head and screams)

                    Long live the king!
SCHAFMAN *(In the cage)*:
    Es lebe hoch der grosse Peer![29]

Act Five

Aboard a ship in the North Sea off the coast of Norway. Sunset. Stormy weather. Peer Gynt, a heavyset old man with steel gray hair and beard, stands aft of the cabin. He's dressed somewhat like a seaman, in a jacket and tall boots. The clothes are a little worn and worse for wear; he himself is weather-beaten and has a harder expression. The ship's captain stands beside the wheel, next to the helmsman. The crew is forward.

PEER GYNT *(Leaning on his arms against the rail and staring at the shore)*:

Look at those mountains! Old man Halling in the sun,
Showing off all his winter clothes. Behind
Stands little brother, Jokle[30]—he's not yet begun
To shed his coat of ice—he doesn't mind
The cold! And Folgefonn[31]—she's a delight
To these old eyes—a virgin dressed in white
Linen. Old-timers, don't get swept away!
You're gentlemen! Besides, your heads are gray.

CAPTAIN *(Shouting forward)*:

Ahoy there! Hoist the lamp—and two men at the wheel!

PEER GYNT:
　　It's a stiff wind.

CAPTAIN:
　　　　　　　There'll be a storm tonight.

PEER GYNT:
　　Is that the Ronde mountain that I see?

CAPTAIN:
　　　　　　　No, she'll
　　Appear shortly—right now she's out of sight.

PEER GYNT:
　　That's Blaho?[32]

CAPTAIN:
　　　　　　　No, but climb up in the rig
　　And you'll catch sight of Galdhopiggen's[33] crest.

PEER GYNT:
　　Where is Harteigen?[34]

CAPTAIN *(Points)*:
　　　　　　　I think it's the big
　　One there.

PEER GYNT:
　　　　　　　Ah!

CAPTAIN:
　　　　　　　You know this country—I'm impressed.

PEER GYNT:
　　It's curious what our memories retain.
　　Just as the proverb says, the dregs remain.

(Spits and stares at the coast)

　　There, where it's getting dark along the mountain pass,
　　Or in these valleys, close and black as ditches—
　　Along the open fjord, or perched on a crevasse—
　　That is where all these stubborn sons-of-bitches
　　Live.

(Looks at the Captain)

No, it's not too crowded here.

CAPTAIN:

That's right—
The villages are few and far between.

PEER GYNT:

Will we put in by sunrise?

CAPTAIN:

Well, we might;
But only if the weather's not too mean.

PEER GYNT:

Those western skies look chancy—

CAPTAIN:

Yes, they do.

PEER GYNT:

Remind me—when we settle our account—
To give a little extra for the crew.
My pleasure, as they say.

CAPTAIN:

Thanks.

PEER GYNT:

Won't amount
To much. I struck gold once, then took a fall;
Fate and I squabbled, had to bid farewell
To one another; what's on board is all
That I possess. The rest went straight to hell.

CAPTAIN:

It's still enough to make your presence known
Among the folks back home.

PEER GYNT:

I have no family.
There won't be any rice or ribbons thrown

At this old geezer at the dock, I guarantee—

CAPTAIN:

Here comes the storm!

PEER GYNT:

                   So Captain, bear in mind,

If someone's in a sticky situation,

You send him straight to me—no hesitation.

CAPTAIN:

It's good of you. They're always in a bind.

With wives and kids—I'm sure you know the way

It is. A seaman's wages don't provide

Much extra, so a bit from you beside

Their pay would make a happy holiday.

PEER GYNT:

What? They have kids, do they? And an old lady!

They're married?

CAPTAIN:

               Yes, they're married—every one

Of them. The cook is practically undone

By poverty and hunger—any aid he

Gets will be welcome.

PEER GYNT:

               Married! Someone's waiting

For them? Who's happy when they come?

CAPTAIN:

               That's right—

The way poor people do.

PEER GYNT:

               He lands one night,

Then what?

CAPTAIN:

               A special dinner, celebrating

His safe return.

PEER GYNT:

                    A candle will be lit?

CAPTAIN:

    Oh, maybe even two; also a bit
    Of schnapps.

PEER GYNT:

                    Well! Sitting by the fire? A boy
    Astride the knee? A room that's full of joy
    And happiness, as well as so much carefree
    Laughter that no one hears a thing.

CAPTAIN:

                    That may be.
    That's why it was so good of you to say
    That you'd—

PEER GYNT *(Hitting the rail)*:

                    What do you think me, anyway—
    A fool? You think that I will spend my money
    On other people's brats? Ha! Ha! That's funny!
    For what I have, I've worked my fingers to the bone!
    But no one's waiting up for poor old Peer!

CAPTAIN:

    As you wish! It's your money—I don't care!

PEER GYNT:

    Right! It belongs to me! It's mine and mine alone!
    As soon as we drop anchor, you produce my bill!
    Passage from Panama, and my ship's store
    Account! Booze for the crew—and nothing more!
    If I give more, then strike me dead! Damned if I will!

CAPTAIN:

    I owe you a receipt, not discipline.
    Excuse me, now. The storm is moving in.

(He walks forward on the deck. It's getting dark; a lamp is lit in the cabin. The sea is getting heavier. Fog and threatening skies)

PEER GYNT:

> They have a bunch of brats at home, do they?
> Whom they recall with love and sympathy,
> Warming their memories each time they weigh
> Anchor! While no one ever thinks of me.
> A candle? Well, I'll put their candles out.
> I'll think of something—Bastards! How about
> Getting them drunk? So drunk that they can't stand
> Straight when they greet their happy little families!
> They'll swear, throw furniture around, backhand
> Their smiling faces—then we'll see how happy these
> Reunions are! The mother running from
> The house, her brats in hand—all her joy come
> To dust!

(The ship is listing heavily; he falls and has difficulty getting a handhold)

> That was a pleasant little ride.
> The ocean's working overtime. Yes, I'd
> Forgot these northern seas—they take delight
> In showing off their willfulness and spite—

(Listening)

> What was that shout?

WATCHMAN *(Up front)*:

> Wreck on the lee!

CAPTAIN *(Amidship, shouting commands)*:

> Rudder to starboard! Close to the wind!

FIRST MATE:

> Are there survivors?

WATCHMAN:

I see three!

PEER GYNT:

Lower a boat!

CAPTAIN:

Not in this sea!

(He moves forward)

PEER GYNT:

Don't think about it!

(To some of the crew)

If you're men, go get
Them! So your fur might get a little wet!

BO'SUN:

In waves like these? The boat would soon be hurled
Against the rocks.

PEER GYNT:

Another shout! Hey, look,
The wind is dying down—I'll pay you, cook!

COOK:

No, not for all the money in the world!

PEER GYNT:

You dogs! You cowards! How canst thou forsake
Thy fellow man? Their children's hearts will break!
Wives wait for them—

BO'SUN:

Patience is good for you.

CAPTAIN:

Watch out—that wave!

FIRST MATE:

It's overturned—onto
Its side.

PEER GYNT:
> So still!

BO'SUN:
> If any of that trio
> Were married, someone just became a widow.

(The storm increases. Peer Gynt is walking on the afterdeck)

PEER GYNT:
> You can't find a believer anywhere
> These days—Christian or any other nomenclature;
> There's no such thing as a good deed, no prayer,
> No one will even show respect for Mother Nature.
> In storms like this, Our Lord is dangerous.
> This cook should watch himself—whom he affronts—
> For you don't play around with elephants—
> But he was openly contemptuous!
> My conscience, though, is clear. When I was called upon—
> And there are witnesses—I volunteered hard-won
> Savings, but what's the good? Clichés abound
> Alleging that good conscience makes soft pillows.
> Oh, sure, maybe when you are on dry ground;
> At sea, that's not worth much—when all around
> Are miscreants, your little peccadillos
> Become entwined with theirs! If there's a wreck,
> You slide with all the others off the deck!
> You're not yourself! The bo'sun's time has come—
> The cook's—then I must march to that same drum!
> You're no more individual than a mouse—
> You're like a sausage in a slaughterhouse!
> Want to know my mistake? I was too meek.
> So all I've gotten is ingratitude.
> If I were young, I'd try a new technique

And be a bit more pushy. Attitude
Is everything. But there's still time—why not?
Peer Gynt is back and flying high, is what
I want them all to think. By hook or crook,
I'll get the farm, and all the rest they took.
But none of them will get inside the parlor!
No! They can stand in line, and let them snarl or
Smile, but they still will have to beg—in vain,
For they won't get a solitary grain
From me. Fate horsewhipped *me*, my friends, ergo,
I have the right to beat on those below—

THE STRANGE PASSENGER *(Standing in the darkness next to Peer Gynt and giving him a friendly greeting)*:
Good evening!

PEER GYNT:
                    Good evening! How did—? Who are you?

THE STRANGE PASSENGER:
I am your fellow passenger, my son.

PEER GYNT:
Really? I thought I was the only one.

THE STRANGE PASSENGER:
An assumption you should now, perhaps, review.

PEER GYNT:
Isn't it strange we didn't meet until
This evening—

THE STRANGE PASSENGER:
                    No, I don't appear in daytime.

PEER GYNT:
You don't look well—white as a sheet! You're ill?

THE STRANGE PASSENGER:
Thank you for asking, but I'm pleased to say I'm
Feeling just fine.

PEER GYNT:
                    It's quite a storm!
THE STRANGE PASSENGER:
                              Divine!

PEER GYNT:
     Divine?
THE STRANGE PASSENGER:
                    The waves are higher than the roof.
     My mouth is watering! Oh, it's a fine
     Evening for shipwrecks! Disappointment-proof!
     And all those bodies floating in the brine!
PEER GYNT:
     Dear God!
THE STRANGE PASSENGER:
                    You ever see one that was strangled—
     Or hanged—or drowned?
PEER GYNT:
                    My nerves are getting jangled—!
THE STRANGE PASSENGER:
     They look as if they're laughing. But among
     My colleagues—we feel that it's forced. The tongue
     Is often bitten through.
PEER GYNT:
                              Not one more sound
     From you!
THE STRANGE PASSENGER:
                    Just this! If we should run aground,
     Go under in the dark—
PEER GYNT:
                              You think we might?
THE STRANGE PASSENGER:
     One really can't be sure on such a night.

Let's say you suffer some paralysis
And drown.

PEER GYNT:

        What?

THE STRANGE PASSENGER:

           Merely a hypothesis.
They say a man with one foot in the grave
Becomes magnanimous and entertains—

PEER GYNT *(Reaches in his pocket)*:

Ah! Money!

THE STRANGE PASSENGER:

        No, no, no! But if you gave
Me legal rights to your esteemed remains—

PEER GYNT:

You've gone too far!

THE STRANGE PASSENGER:

          Only the corpse, you see,
For science sake!

PEER GYNT:

        You get away from me!

THE STRANGE PASSENGER:

My dear man, think about it—you would be
Most carefully dissected and displayed.
I'm looking for the seat of dreams, you see,
But nothing in your innards would evade—

PEER GYNT:

Go!

THE STRANGE PASSENGER:

      But a drowned, blue corpse—not even warm!

PEER GYNT:

Your blasphemy is what brought on this storm!
An outrage! This is no way to behave!
This is a storm that almost advertises

It wants to put us in a watery grave,
And here you stand imploring—"Please, capsize us!"

THE STRANGE PASSENGER:

You're not in a negotiating mood
But time, I think, may change your attitude.

(Waving goodbye in a friendly manner)

We'll meet when you are going under, sir,
Or earlier, of course, if you prefer.

(Goes into the cabin)

PEER GYNT:

Horrible creatures—all these wretched academics!
Freethinker! Atheist!

(To the Bo'sun, walking by)

Hey, bo'sun, who
Is the passenger? Where do you get all these eccentrics?

BO'SUN:

There isn't any passenger but you.

PEER GYNT:

There's no one? This is getting worse and worse.

(To a Seaman, coming out of the cabin)

Who just went in that door?

SEAMAN *(Passing by)*:

The dog!

WATCHMAN *(Shouting)*:

Ahoy!

Land dead ahead!

PEER GYNT:

My bag! My strong box! Curse
You! Bring them up!

BO'SUN:

I've things to do, old boy!

PEER GYNT:

Captain, my little joke aside, if cash
Would save the cook, I'm happy to help out—

CAPTAIN:

The jib is down!

FIRST MATE:

The foresail, too! About!

About!

BO'SUN *(Forward, calling out)*:

Land on the bow!

CAPTAIN:

She's going to crash!

(The ship crashes. Noise and confusion)

Off the coast, rocks and surf. The ship is going down. Through the fog, we see a dinghy with two men aboard. A large wave swamps it; it capsizes; we hear shouts; afterward, everything is quiet. Finally, the overturned boat appears. Peer Gynt comes up near it.

PEER GYNT:

Help! Help! A lifeboat! God! I'll drown!
Be with me as the Good Book says you'll be!

(Clings to the upturned keel)

COOK *(Appearing on the other side)*:

Oh, God, help me—I'm going down!
My little ones! Oh Lord—mercy on me!

(Grabbing the keel)

PEER GYNT:

Let go!

COOK:

Let go!

PEER GYNT:

I'll hit you!

COOK:

I'll hit back!

PEER GYNT:

Let go, you clod! I'll kick you till you're black
And blue! This wreck can't carry two!

COOK:

That's right! So swim!

PEER GYNT:

You swim!

COOK:

Screw you!

(They fight; one of the Cook's hands is crippled; he holds on with the other one)

PEER GYNT:

Let go that hand!

COOK:

Sir, help me, please!
Remember all my little ones!

PEER GYNT:

I haven't any legatees,
I need to live to have some sons!

COOK:

Please, sir, let go! I'm young, you're old!

PEER GYNT:

Oh, hurry up and drown, man—you're too big!

COOK:

    Be merciful! I can't keep hold
    Much longer! No one waits for you, you pig!

(Screams and lets go)

    I'm drowning! Sir!
PEER GYNT *(Grabs him)*:

                    Why do I bother?
    I got you! Now say the Our Father!
COOK:

    I can't remember anything!
PEER GYNT:

    The high points, then! Stop gibbering!
COOK:

    Give us this day—
PEER GYNT:

                  Skip all that. Look,
    Get to the part where you've done wrong.
COOK:

    Give us this day—
PEER GYNT:

                  The same old song!
    It's obvious you were a cook.

(Loses his grip)

COOK *(Going under)*:
    Give us this day—

    (Disappears)

PEER GYNT:

                  Amen, my friend!
    True to yourself until the end.

(Clambers on to the overturned keel)

Where there is life, they say, there's hope—
THE STRANGE PASSENGER *(Grabbing hold of the boat)*:
Good morning!
PEER GYNT:
         Uhh!
THE STRANGE PASSENGER:
               I thought I heard a cry—
What fun to have you in my scope
Again. Well? Was I right, or wasn't I?
PEER GYNT:
Let go! There's barely room for *me*!
THE STRANGE PASSENGER:
I'm paddling with my legs, don't worry!
I'll hold on very gingerly—
One fingertip. You're in a hurry,
I know, but apropos the stiff—
PEER GYNT:
Quiet!
THE STRANGE PASSENGER:
         It's almost over—if—
PEER GYNT:
Shut up!
THE STRANGE PASSENGER:
         All right! It's all the same
To me.

(Quiet)

PEER GYNT:
         What now?

THE STRANGE PASSENGER:
                    Shh.

PEER GYNT:

                         Hell of a game—

     What are you doing?

THE STRANGE PASSENGER:
                    Waiting.

PEER GYNT *(Pulling his hair)*:

                              I'll go mad!

     And what are you?

THE STRANGE PASSENGER *(Nodding)*:
                    A friend.

PEER GYNT:

                    Obscene!

THE STRANGE PASSENGER:

                         My son,

     What do you think? Haven't you ever had
     Acquaintances like me?

PEER GYNT:

                    The Evil One!

THE STRANGE PASSENGER *(Softly)*:

     Is it his habit, friend, to light a candle
     And lead you gently through life's darkest night?

PEER GYNT:

     I see! Well, now you've given me a handle
     On it. You are a messenger of light?

THE STRANGE PASSENGER:

     My dear sir, have you—even *once* a year—
     Experienced anxiety or fear?

PEER GYNT:

     When I am threatened, I'm afraid—of course—
     But that's not what you mean—this is some Morse
     Code that I—

THE STRANGE PASSENGER:
> Have you *once* in life—now hear
> Me!—been victorious despite your fear?

PEER GYNT *(Giving him a look)*:
> If you have come to open up a door
> For me, you're late—you should have come before.
> You could not choose a more ridiculous
> Terrain! These waves can't wait to swallow us.

THE STRANGE PASSENGER:
> Would feelings of exhilaration be
> More heartfelt in the peace and harmony
> Of your own home?

PEER GYNT:
> Stop it—you're being clever!
> Do you believe that repartee could ever
> Open my eyes?

THE STRANGE PASSENGER:
> Where I'm from, comedy
> And pathos are respected equally.

PEER GYNT:
> Everything has its place—the clergyman
> Should not be treated like the publican.

THE STRANGE PASSENGER:
> It doesn't follow—you know—*a priori*
> That just because you're dead you wore *cothurni*.

PEER GYNT:
> Get thee behind me, demon! Please! No more!
> I don't want to die! I want to go ashore!

THE STRANGE PASSENGER:
> Oh, *please*, no need to fret—matter of fact,
> You can't die—it's the middle of the act.

(Slips away)

PEER GYNT:

>He could have said that sooner, in my eyes;
>But no, he wanted time to moralize.

*Churchyard in a village high in the mountains. Funeral procession.
The minister and the villagers. The last hymn is being sung. Peer
Gynt walks by on the road.*

PEER GYNT *(At the gate)*:

>One more who goes the way of all flesh, I see.
>All I can say is: thank God it's not me.

(Steps inside)

MINISTER *(Speaking beside the grave)*:

>   Now, as his soul receives the judgment of God
>And dust is settling on the broken pod
>Of his remains, let's speak a word or two
>Of the departed's journey here on earth.
>He wasn't erudite, or well-to-do,
>And his opinions were of little worth
>Because his stature and his voice were weak.
>He never got his way—it was a great frustration—
>Even in his own home. In church, he'd seek
>Permission just to sit among the congregation.
>   As you all know, he came to us from Gudbrandsdal
>When he was just a boy. And then on Sundays—
>The only day we saw him—how it struck us all
>That he would keep his right hand in his pocket—always.
>   His right hand in his pocket was the telling

Element in the portrait of the man,
Along with his embarrassment, compelling
A speech to end before the speech began.
        Why did he stay on his own quiet course,
Avoiding us? He didn't think we'd understand
Why there were but four fingers on that unseen hand.
His problem wasn't shyness, but remorse.
        One day in Lunde—many years ago—
The army searched for troops to fill its quota.
A wartime spirit reigned from Minnesota
To Norway; not a man was saying no.
        At a large table sat a Captain, flanked
By sergeants and the sheriff. I was there
As well. Boy after boy—in underwear—
Was measured and accepted. Each one thanked
The Captain, dressed, and then went out the door.
Outside, happy and loud, were many more.
        A name was called. I saw a new boy enter,
Pale as a glacier in the coldest winter.
"Come closer, son," one of the sergeants muttered;
He did; one hand was wrapped in rags; his head
Kept dropping lower as he gasped and stuttered;
He wouldn't speak, no matter what they said
Or ordered him to do. The Captain slapped
Him finally. That's when he made the claim
His scythe had slipped, and then with cheeks aflame,
He showed his hand and said, "That's why it's wrapped."
        Immediately the room went deathly still.
Some were exchanging glances—they would kill
Him in a minute if their looks were stones.
He didn't see their hate, but in his bones
He felt it. Then the Captain, staid and slow,
Stood up and spit, pointed and whispered, "Go!"

The watchers, parting to both sides, had made
A road that led straight out the door. He left,
And flew as thieves fly following the theft;
And when he reached the mountain, up he ran
Showering those below with a cascade
Of stones. Up there, the boy could be a man.
        Half a year later he returned—the bitterness
Had passed—with mother, baby and intended—
And leased some land that had been recommended
To him—away from us—next to the wilderness.
He soon was married, and he built a home.
He placed his farmland under cultivation;
Then, before long, thanks to his dedication,
His fields were gold as far as eyes could roam.
One hand was hidden on the Sabbath day,
But weekdays those nine fingers must have been
As hard at work as other peoples' ten.
Then the Spring floods washed everything away.
        They barely stayed alive. Drained and dejected,
He set himself to work clearing his land once more,
And smoke was curling from his chimney long before
The Fall. The house was high, better protected
This time. Protected? From the floods, perchance,
But two years later came an avalanche.
        This man could not be crushed; he was unfazed.
He dug, he cleaned, he cleared the rock and grime—
Before next winter's snow was gone, he raised
A modest roof a third and final time.
He had three school-age sons, this hardy man,
All ready to begin attending classes—
Traversing many dangerous mountain passes,
Though, just to reach the point where roads began.
What did he do? The oldest one was on his own,

Muddling through as best be could, and when the track
Got treacherous, father would see a rope was thrown.
The other two? One in his arms, one on his back.

That's how he toiled year after year, until
These three were grown and could repay the favor.
Three wealthy men in the new world now savor
The fruits of learning; father's waiting still.

He wasn't a farsighted man. Beyond
Those close to him was nothing. Words that tell
Upon our hearts, that forge for us a bond,
Were meaningless to him, a clanging bell—
The soul, the fatherland, ideas of any size
Seemed to be so much fog before his narrowed eyes.

But oh, he knew about humility, this man;
He bore the condemnation of that drafting day
In Lunde palpably—as in the blush that ran
Across his cheeks, the hand that he kept tucked away.
A criminal? Outside the law? Maybe!
But one thing stands and shines above the law,
As Glittertinden's[35] peak will certainly
Be dwarfed by morning clouds, just as we saw
Today. Was he a model citizen?
Probably not, in the eyes of church or state.
But in his home, he left this benison:
He was himself. And there, this man was great.
The bell rang true in life that rang at birth—
Although the sound was dampened. We cannot
But wish him now a soldier's peace, who fought
And fell in the farmer's war against the earth.

It's not for us to look into his heart—
That is a task for the shepherd, not a part
For sheep—but as he goes to his reward,
Let's pray that he's not lame before His Lord.

(The procession breaks up; they leave. Peer Gynt remains)

PEER GYNT:

Well, *that's* what I call Christianity!
Nothing unpleasant to get in the way;
Nevertheless, what pastor had to say—
To be yourself despite adversity—
Is one commandment that we must obey.

(Looks into the grave)

When I was in the forest chopping wood,
A boy cut off his finger as I stood
And watched. Was this the one? Who knows! If I
Weren't standing here—with stick in hand—close by
This grave, I might think it was *I* who slept,
I who was praised, and over whom they wept.
Yes, isn't it a nice formality
To look back in respectful memory
And Christian charity at days gone by.
It wouldn't bother me at all if my
Eulogy were in this man's hands—he's blessed
With fitting dignity. However, I
Don't want to be the undertaker's guest
Just yet! And, as they say, "That's for the best."
Or, "I'll cross that bridge when I come to it."
Also, "It's not my funeral!" True, it
Will happen someday, and the church will be
My comfort. I was not appreciative enough
Before; but now I see, when times are getting tough,
How good it is to hear—repeatedly—
"As you have sown, so you shall reap." You see,
You have to be true to yourself alone!
Care only for yourself and what you own!
Then even if bad luck should come, I still can reach

The end able to say, "I practice what I preach!"
I'm off! Yes, let the road be straight and narrow,
Let fate be scornful and contemptuous,
Old Peer Gynt trudges on, straight as an arrow,
He may be poor, but he is virtuous.

(He leaves)

*Hillside with a dried out riverbed. A mill on the riverside, in ruins;
the land is neglected; disrepair all around. Above, a large farm
where there is an auction. A crowd of villagers. Drinking and
commotion. Peer Gynt is sitting on a pile of rocks at the mill site.*

PEER GYNT:

It's just as far, forward or back;
Outside or in looks just as black.
Time marches on; the river wears away
Its bed. Go 'round, the Great Between would say.

MAN DRESSED IN BLACK:

It's trash! Everything good's been sold or tossed.

(Coming upon Peer Gynt)

A stranger here? God bless you, friend! You lost?

PEER GYNT:

This is a quite impressive show of mirth!
Greetings! Is it a wedding or a birth?

MAN DRESSED IN BLACK:

Homecoming would be a more dignified
Description. Worms are welcoming the bride.

PEER GYNT:

And fighting for the morsels that remain.

MAN DRESSED IN BLACK:

    The song is over—end of the refrain.

PEER GYNT:

    Each song has the exact same ending.

    I knew them all, but now they're blending

    Together.

A MAN OF TWENTY *(With a casting ladle)*:

              That's it! Everything is sold!

    Peer Gynt used this, the story goes, to mold

    His silver buttons!

ANOTHER ONE:

              Peer Gynt's purse! I paid a penny!

A THIRD:

    The basket for his coins, if ever he had any!

PEER GYNT:

    Peer Gynt? Who's he?

MAN DRESSED IN BLACK:

              A relative, or so

    I'm told, of the deceased—that's all I know—

    And Aslak, too.

A MAN DRESSED IN GRAY:

              You drunk? Don't forget me!

MAN DRESSED IN BLACK:

    Would we forget the pantry door? Would we?

MAN DRESSED IN GRAY:

    Oh, yeah! It didn't seem to bother you.

MAN DRESSED IN BLACK:

    I wonder how the hell she'll try to screw

    The Grim Reaper.

MAN DRESSED IN GRAY:

            We're all one happy family,

    Brother! Drink up!

MAN DRESSED IN BLACK:

> That's drunken drivel! Damn me
> If I'm your brother!

MAN DRESSED IN GRAY:

> Blood is like a fingerprint;
> We have a common relative, you know—Peer Gynt!

(They go off together)

PEER GYNT *(Softly)*:

> It seems that we're renewing friendships.

A BOY *(Shouting at the Man Dressed in Black)*:

> My dead mother
> Is going to get you, Aslak! Drunkard! Sure as hell!

PEER GYNT *(Gets up)*:

> Here the old adage doesn't seem to work. In other
> Words, stirring up the stink just makes a better smell.

A BOY *(With a bearskin)*:

> The Dovre cat![36] The skin at least. Sir, I believe
> He was the one who chased the trolls on Christmas Eve.

ANOTHER *(With a reindeer skull)*:

> Here is the giant buck that carried Peer
> Across the Gjendin ridge—flew through the air.

A THIRD *(With a hammer, calling after the Man Dressed in Black)*:

> Aslak! Remember? Isn't this the hammer
> You crushed the shell with? And it made you stammer?

A FOURTH *(Empty-handed)*:

> Mads Moen, look! The cloak Ingrid and Peer
> Were wearing when they vanished in thin air!

PEER GYNT:

> Give me a swig, my friend! I'm feeling old.
> I want to auction off some junk I hold
> In my possession.

A BOY:

Yeah? Like what?

PEER GYNT:

Oh, I've

A castle in the Ronde.

THE BOY:

Sakes alive!

I bid a button!

PEER GYNT:

How about a drink?

Anything less would be a sin.

ANOTHER BOY:

I think

This old coot's funny!

(They're all gathering around him)

PEER GYNT *(Calling out)*:

Blackie, that's my horse!

Who makes an offer?

ONE OF THEM:

Can he run?

PEER GYNT:

Of course!

Into the sunset, boys! That nag can fly

As fast—as fast as old Peer Gynt could lie.

VOICES:

What else?

PEER GYNT:

I have some gold, I have some dross!

It's shipwrecked goods—I'm selling at a loss.

A BOY:

Go on!

PEER GYNT:

A dream about a sacred book!

That you can have for just a buttonhook.

THE BOY:

To hell with dreams!

PEER GYNT:

Well, how about my empire?

I'll throw it in the pile—it may inspire

You, too!

THE BOY:

Is there a crown?

PEER GYNT:

Oh, yes—of straw.

It will fit anyone—hurrah, hurrah!

But look! A madman's hair! It's gray! I beg

You—look! A prophet's beard! A rotten egg!

And you can have it all! It's readily bestowed

On him who finds the sign that says, "Here lies the road!"

SHERIFF *(Who has arrived)*:

Keep on this way and your road, without fail,

Will lead directly to the county jail.

PEER GYNT *(Hat in hand)*:

All right! But this Peer Gynt affair—tell me about it.

SHERIFF:

What are you up—

PEER GYNT:

I'm asking nicely!

SHERIFF:

I don't doubt it.

He was some lousy storyteller, so they say.

PEER GYNT:

A storyteller?

SHERIFF:

Yes, he made up everything,

Of course, but it was truthful in *his* reckoning.
Excuse me, I have other things to do today.

(Leaves)

PEER GYNT:

And what's become of this odd fellow now?

AN OLD MAN:

Oh, he went overseas. I don't know how
Or why, but just like all those slippery fellows,
He had a fitting end—upon the gallows.

PEER GYNT:

The gallows? Well! There are some things we can depend
On, eh? He was true to himself right to the end.

(Taking his leave)

Goodbye—and thank you for the splendid day!

(Takes a few steps, then stops)

Would all you lovely lads and lasses like to hear
A story I picked up along the way?

A VOICE:

Of course, but do you know a good one?

PEER GYNT:

Oh, my dear!

(He moves closer; a strange expression seems to light up his face)

I was in San Francisco, prospecting for gold,
When an odd group of clowns and entertainers rolled
Into town. Violins were played by amputees,
Others were doing Spanish dances on their knees,
Another one, or so I'm told, sang a refrain
While someone with a drill bored holes right through his
brain.

The devil thought, then, he would join the party
And try his luck. And what did Mr. Smarty
Pants advertise that he could do? His big
Illusion, friends, was grunting like a pig.
His personality, though overblown,
Filled houses even though he was unknown.
He wore a cape which really was a bit outré,
But *man muss sich drapieren*,[37] as the Germans say.
And no one recognized the pig-like shape
Hidden beneath the huge, luxuriant cape.
The curtain rose, and quiet fell out front.
The devil pinched the pig and made him grunt.
(You see, he thought his act a fantasy
On piggishness, whether confined or free.)
Then came a true slaughterhouse squeal—
The artist bowed, turned on his heel,
And left! The show became notorious;
The critics were, of course, censorious.
One said the actor's voice was unimpressive,
Another found the death scene overdone;
Qua grunt, however—on this everyone
Agreed—the histrionics were excessive.
The moral is: never be confident
That any audience is intelligent.

(He salutes them and leaves. An uneasy silence descends on the crowd)

———————

Whitsun Eve. In the great forest. In the background, in a clearing,
a cabin with reindeer antlers over the door. Peer Gynt is crawling
among the trees, collecting wild onions.

PEER GYNT:

This could be called a point of view. What's next?
Look at your choices, then select your text—
Anyway, that's how I did it—from Caesar
All the way back to old Nebuchadnezzar.
I had to skim the Bible after all;
We come back home to momma—in a crawl—
Just like a baby. Well, it's written: dust thou be-est!
Phooey! The most important thing—even a theist
Would tell you—is to eat! Wild onions, though?
They're not worth much. I'll set some traps, also
Fetch water from the brook—that will take care of thirst;
Among the animals, remember, man's the first.
When death comes—as it will, even to me—
I want to crawl under a fallen tree
Like a cuddly bear, and carve my epitaph
Into the bark—a single paragraph:
Here lies Peer Gynt, a decent fellow now deceased,
Emperor of all other animals, at least.
Emperor?

(Laughs to himself)

Boy, you're cuckoo! When did you become one?
You're not an emperor, Peer Gynt—you are an onion!
And now I'm going to peel you, little Peer!
You think that you're mistreated? I don't care.

(Picks up an onion and tears off one layer after another)

The outside layer's torn—who's that? Oh, yes,
The shipwrecked soul, who's signalling distress.

Passenger skin! It has a sallow tint—
It tastes, however, like the real Peer Gynt.
And inside here must be the old gold digger;
The juice is gone—he never had much vigor.
This heavy peel with the hard overlay
Must be the fur trader at Hudson Bay.
The one beneath looks like a crown—thank you!
We'll discard that without any to-do.
Here's the historian—short, but eloquent.
And here's the prophet, fresh and succulent,
Who stinks, it's written, of so many lies
That honest men get water in their eyes.
This layer, soft and unctuous, must be
The esquire, living so luxuriously.
This! Sick—and streaked with black! It's sinister.
Could be a Negro, or a minister.

(Peels several at once)

An awful lot of layers! More and more!
Come on! When do I reach the inner core?

(Peels the entire onion)

Damned if I do! However far I go
It's only peel—smaller and smaller. Ho!
A little joke of nature!

(Throws the pieces away)

                    Keeps me humble,
I guess. Don't think too much, you're sure to stumble.
That's certainly a possibility
But *I'm* as well-protected as can be
On all fours.

(Scratches his neck)

        Funny—what a wild goose chase!
Life, as it's labeled, always holds the ace
In the hole. Whether a man will bet or bluff—
No matter what he has—it's not enough!

(He has approached the cabin, discovers it and stops)

That cabin in the clearing! Huh!

(Rubs his eyes)

        It seems
Familiar, doesn't it! One of my dreams?
The antlers on the gable . . . decoration!
A mermaid—modest in configuration!
Lies! There's no mermaid! Nails and boards cannot—!
No lock can stop a furious demon thought!

SOLVEIG *(In the cabin, singing)*:
    Now I'm prepared for Whitsun Eve,
    And I believe you're coming, my boy,
    You're coming, I believe.
    And if you have a heavy load
    That makes you late
    Then I will wait
    As I promised—here, at the end of the road.

PEER GYNT *(Standing quietly, pale as death)*:
    One who remembered, one who forgot.
    One who is lost, and one who is not.
    There is no second chance—ah, it is clear!
    My one and only empire—oh, it was *here*!

(Runs along the forest path)

Night. A pine grove. Fire has destroyed the trees. Blackened trunks all around. Patches of white fog on the forest floor. Peer Gynt runs through the grove.

PEER GYNT:

Ashes and mist, dust in the wind,
Materials with which to build!
The stench inside of one who sinned;
A whited sepulchre—self-willed!
Poems and dreams and stillborn realizations
Are what make up the pyramid's foundations;
And over that the work will rise
Upon a scaffolding of lies.
Avoid regret! Escape! will read
The banner at the top. To make it
Clear, doomsday trumpets bruit the creed
Of *Petrus Gyntus Caesar fecit*!

(Listens)

A child that's crying? What's that sound?
It's almost crying, almost song—
Tumbleweed rolling all around!

(Kicking)

Off the road! Back where you belong!

TUMBLEWEED *(On the ground)*:

We are your thoughts;
You should have thought us—
Wee little tots—
You should have taught us!

PEER GYNT *(Walking around)*:

I did give life! I got the dregs!
Yes, a bad seed with crooked legs!

TUMBLEWEED:

>   We're meant to lift
>   Our voice, to rouse, to lead—
>   Here we must drift
>   As withered tumbleweed

PEER GYNT *(Trips)*:

>   Tumbleweed, eh? You little pup!
>   Don't try to trip your father up!

(Runs away)

DEAD LEAVES *(Windblown)*:

>   We are solutions;
>   You should have found us!
>   Your dissolutions
>   Have aged and browned us.
>   The worms have eaten us
>   All the way through;
>   The wind has beaten us
>   Down—where were you?

PEER GYNT:

>   Let me become your fond advisor—
>   Drop dead! You'll make good fertilizer.

A MOANING WIND:

>   I am the song
>   That never was sung.
>   I lay for so long
>   On the tip of your tongue.
>   I lay for so long
>   Awaiting your choice
>   That wrong repaid wrong—
>   I poisoned your voice!

PEER GYNT:

>   Poison your little poem, you! Listen to *him*! Damn!

Did I have time for verses and that kind of flimflam?

(Tries a shortcut)

DROPS OF DEW *(Falling from the branches)*:
We are all of the tears
That never were shed.
We'd have melted your fears
And dissolved your dread.
We were lying in wait,
But now it's too late;
We never were found
Now your heart is icebound—

PEER GYNT:
Thanks! In the Ronde I let out a wail
Or two! What did I get? Knocked on my tail!

BROKEN STRAWS:
We are your inventions;
You should have conceived us!
Doubt and inattention
Silenced and deceived us.
On the last day
When justice will prevail,
We'll have our say—
Then watch your face turn pale!

PEER GYNT:
A dirty trick to play on anyone!
To condemn a man for what he *hasn't* done!

(Hurries away)

AASE'S VOICE *(In the distance)*:
That is no way to drive!
You almost turned us over! Phooey!
I swear I won't survive.
Do we have far to go, Peer? Do we?

This isn't the right way!
Where is the castle?
The devil led you astray
With the stick and the tassel!

PEER GYNT:

I think I'd best be on the run.
If all the sins the Evil One
Commits are on my back, I'll fall.
My own, God knows, are hardly small.

(Runs)

Another place on the moor.

PEER GYNT *(Singing)*:

Gravedigger! Gravedigger! Where are you?
The sexton's bleating hallelu!
Tie a black band around your hat—
We're chasing the dead; just fancy that!

(The Button Molder appears on a side road, carrying a tool box and a large casting ladle)

BUTTON MOLDER:

Greetings!

PEER GYNT:

Good evening, friend!

BUTTON MOLDER:

Unless I err
Our man is in a hurry. Where to, sir?

PEER GYNT:

A wake.

BUTTON MOLDER:

Really? Forgive me if I stare,
But please—would you by any chance be Peer?

PEER GYNT:

Peer Gynt is how they say it.

BUTTON MOLDER:

Is that right?
It is Peer Gynt whom I'm to meet tonight.

PEER GYNT:

You are? What do you want?

BUTTON MOLDER:

Well, without more ado—
I am a button molder—you're to go into
My melting spoon.

PEER GYNT:

What for?

BUTTON MOLDER:

To be redone.

PEER GYNT:

Redone?

BUTTON MOLDER:

Here 'tis—waiting for you, my son.
Your coffin's ordered and your grave prepared.
The worms are waiting for your corpse below—
I'm to collect your soul, Master declared,
Immediately, or even sooner.

PEER GYNT:

No!
Impossible! Without a bit of warning?

BUTTON MOLDER:

I fear that with a wake or birth
We often choose the day without informing
The guest of honor here on earth.

PEER GYNT:

    Right. I forget these things as I get older.
    And you're—?

BUTTON MOLDER:

              Didn't you hear? A button molder.

PEER GYNT:

    Oh, sure. A rose by any other name—!
    So, Peer, *that* is where you're to go! But this
    Is not according to the rules—and shame
    On you! I don't deserve this ruthlessness!
    I'm really not as bad as I've been branded.
    I've done some good—a bit of a beginner,
    But trying! Maybe I've been heavy-handed,
    But you could never say I was a sinner!

BUTTON MOLDER:

    But *that* is just the problem, don't you see?
    You're not a sinner who will make girls swoon,
    You understand; therefore, you needn't be
    Tormented. You go in the melting spoon,
    With lots of others!

PEER GYNT:

              Call it what you want—
    Lager or bock—they both are beers! Don't lie!
    Get thee behind me, Satan!

BUTTON MOLDER:

              I'll be blunt—
    I am chagrined by that! You think that I
    Would run around on hooves?

PEER GYNT:

             Oh, hooves or claws,
    Who cares! Just watch yourself! And stay away
    From me!

BUTTON MOLDER:

    My friend, you're grasping now at straws.
There's not a lot of time. I'd like to say
Something to you about how matters stand.
You haven't done anything in the sinning
Department—you confess—one could call grand
Or even average—

PEER GYNT:

        Now you're beginning
To make some sense.

BUTTON MOLDER:

        Wait just a minute, please.
To call you virtuous would be too much. I've seen—

PEER GYNT:

 I never claimed to be Diogenes!

BUTTON MOLDER:

 So—fair to middling, one might say. Or in between!
No, really decent sinners I don't meet
Too much these days. We lack the discipline.
It's not enough to wear your clothes and eat
And sleep—you have to concentrate to sin
Effectively.

PEER GYNT:

     You made your point—quite rightly.
One has to carry on like a fanatic.

BUTTON MOLDER:

 You have, however, taken sinning lightly.

PEER GYNT:

 A splash of mud! I was—at worst!—erratic.

BUTTON MOLDER:

 Now we see eye to eye. The sulphurous pond
Is not for those who splash in puddles here and there.

PEER GYNT:

And so I'm free to go, as we are fond—

BUTTON MOLDER:

And so you will be melted down, my dearest Peer.

PEER GYNT:

What kind of tricks have you come up with since
I've been away from home?

BUTTON MOLDER:

The custom is as old
As Genesis—or as old as the Prince
Of Darkness—it's meant to protect the Master's gold
And precious ores. You know the craft a bit—
A casting can turn out—frankly—like shit.
A button, for example, might not have a loop.
What would you do?

PEER GYNT:

I'd throw it in the trash.

BUTTON MOLDER:

I see. Well, Jon Gynt was known as the nincompoop
Who threw away bushels and bushels of cash.
My Master, though, is frugal—a more healthy
Attitude; so, of course, he is a wealthy
Man—who would never deem unusable
Something that could be raw material.
You were intended, Peer, to be a shining
Button on mankind's coat, but something went
Awry. Obviously, you need refining.
Upon reflection, it is our intent
To merge you with the masses.

PEER GYNT:

What? You couldn't mean
You're going to make me into something new
By mixing me with Tom and Dick, and—

BUTTON MOLDER:
                         Oh, we've seen
    It work with many others just like you.
    They do the same thing at the mint with money
    That has been worn or frayed by circulation.
PEER GYNT:
    This is so stingy it's not even funny!
    Frugality! This is annihilation!
    Buttons without a loop, worn money—*that's* the whole
    Of his concern? That isn't worth a snap
    Of someone's fingers!
BUTTON MOLDER:
                              Since he's given you a soul
    You have a certain value, sir, as scrap.
PEER GYNT:
    No! I say no! I'll fight you tooth and nail!
    I won't accept it! No! It just won't do!
BUTTON MOLDER:
    What else? Be sensible. Struggle will avail
    You nothing. Heaven's not the place for you—
PEER GYNT:
    I'm modest—I don't aim so high; but say
    That I must lose myself, and I will fight!
    I demand judgment—the old-fashioned way!
    Send me below to That One—Prince of Night—
    A hundred years, if that must be the case!
    Really! I don't think that's so monumental—
    After all, what they say about the place
    Is that the pain is moral—that sounds gentle—
    It's a transition, as it is said somewhere,
    And as the fox said when they skinned him. Yes,
    You simply wait it out, and don't despair,
    And hope for better days. But I confess

This other thing—to disappear inside
A total stranger's body—like a speck!—
This casting ladle thing—this Gynticide!—
Drives me insane. Look! I'm a nervous wreck!

BUTTON MOLDER:

But my dear man, why are you waxing so
Emotional about a little thing?
You've never been yourself at all! Ergo,
Why in the world oppose contributing
To others as you fade away?

PEER GYNT:

                    What? *I've* not been—!
Peer Gynt's been someone else? Don't make me laugh!
No, Mr. Button Molder, you've been taken in.
When they sit down to write my epitaph,
My friend, they'll speak of Peer and only Peer—
How he was nothing less and nothing more!

BUTTON MOLDER:

Impossible! I have my orders. There,
In black and white—"Peer Gynt has heretofore
Not realized the purpose of his birth
And thus he must be melted down anon!"

PEER GYNT:

Bunk! There are lots of other Gynts on earth;
It's someone else! Rasmus, perhaps, or Jon!

BUTTON MOLDER:

Oh, please! I melted them down long ago.
Don't make it hard on me; we're wasting time!

PEER GYNT:

Well, that's too bad! Wouldn't it be a low
Point in the morning when you find that I'm
Not who you wanted, after all! Watch out!
You have a grave responsibility—

BUTTON MOLDER:

I have it here in writing—

PEER GYNT:

How about

Postponing—

BUTTON MOLDER:

Why?

PEER GYNT:

The possibility

That I could prove I was myself throughout
My life, if that's all we're at odds about.

BUTTON MOLDER:

Prove it?

PEER GYNT:

With witnesses—recommendations!

BUTTON MOLDER:

My Master never issues cancellations.

PEER GYNT:

Well, we'll cross that bridge when we come to it!
We have one chance to live—I value it!
I have one self—it can't just melt away!
So loan it to me, sir—short-term! I'll pay
You back soon! Yes? Agreed?

BUTTON MOLDER:

Yes, I agree.

Till the next crossroad only, you are free.

(Peer Gynt runs away)

Elsewhere on the moor.

PEER GYNT *(On a dead run)*:
　　Aah! Time is money, everybody says.
　　Where the hell is the next crossroad? Who knows!
　　Maybe around the corner, maybe Suez!
　　The earth is like a red hot iron—it glows!
　　A witness! Yes, a witness! Where to find
　　One in the woods? I'm going to lose my mind!
　　Is this what you would call fair play—I'm asking you—
　　That an old man must prove what he's entitled to?

(An elderly, stooped man—walking stick in hand, bag over his shoulder—trudges along the path)

OLD MAN *(Stops)*:
　　Could you spare something for a homeless man?
PEER GYNT:
　　Sorry, but I'm in something of a bind—
OLD MAN:
　　Prince Peer! Imagine! After such a span
　　Of time!
PEER GYNT:
　　　　　　　But who—
OLD MAN:
　　　　　　　　　　　Ronde has slipped your mind?
PEER GYNT:
　　You couldn't—
OLD MAN:
　　　　　　　　The Old Man of Dovre—yes!
PEER GYNT:
　　Old Man of Dovre? Well, I'd never guess!
OLD MAN:
　　One might say I've seen better days than these!

PEER GYNT:
    You're ruined?
OLD MAN:
                    On the path straight to the poorhouse;
    They stripped me clean. I'm hungry as a field mouse.
PEER GYNT:
    Hooray! Such witnesses don't grow on trees!
OLD MAN:
    The Prince has also gotten gray; he's wobbling
    A bit.
PEER GYNT:
                    Yes, time has torn my life to tatters.
    Father-in-law, forget these private matters,
    And please—above all else—no family squabbling.
    I was insane back then—
OLD MAN:
                    Ha-ha! Oh, yes,
    The Prince indulged in some youthful excess!
    The Prince was clever, though, to jilt the bride—
    He saved himself from injury and shame;
    Oh, she became a scandal far and wide—
PEER GYNT:
    Aha!
OLD MAN:
                    She made short work of our good name—
    Can you imagine?—she and Trond have tied
    The knot!
PEER GYNT:
                    Which Trond?
OLD MAN:
                    Val Mountain Trond.
PEER GYNT:
                    Oh, no, not him!

Once—long ago—I lured three little cherubim
Away from Trond.

OLD MAN:

My grandson's big and fat,
And he has children following behind—

PEER GYNT:

Yes, my dear man, but let's not talk of that
Right now; there's something pressing on my mind.
I'm in a rather sticky situation;
I need a reference—a recommendation.
So if you think that you could help me out,
I'm sure that I could find a little change—

OLD MAN:

My stars! The Prince needs me? Well, turn about
Is fair play, right? Perhaps we could arrange
A trade of references.

PEER GYNT:

That's even better.
I'm short of cash; I'd rather write a letter.
But here's my problem—you remember how
We met—the night I saw the dancing cow?

OLD MAN:

Of course, my Prince!

PEER GYNT:

Will you please stop this prince-ing?
You threatened me—said you would cut my eye
And change me to a troll. I don't know why,
But somehow you thought that would be convincing.
But I did what? Did I beg or entreat?
No! I swore I'd stand on my own two feet!
I gave up all—the power and the glory
And love—to be myself. Now that's the story
I would like you to give in testimony—

OLD MAN:
    I can't.
PEER GYNT:
              What do you mean? What is this—blackmail?
OLD MAN:
    I couldn't swear to that! It's false! It's phony!
    You do recall that you put on a troll's tail
    And drank our mead—
PEER GYNT:
                        Oh, well, you tempted me,
    But I put up tremendous opposition—
    And *that's* how one should judge integrity.
    The final verse of any composition
    Is what should count.
OLD MAN:
                        Agreed! So why the fuss?
PEER GYNT:
    What do you mean?
OLD MAN:
                        The night that you left us
    Our slogan was emblazoned on your heart.
PEER GYNT:
    What's that?
OLD MAN:
              That segregating word, friend—tough
    But true.
PEER GYNT:
              What word?
OLD MAN:
                        One that sets trolls apart
    From man—To thine own self be true *enough*!
PEER GYNT *(Steps back)*:
    Enough!

OLD MAN:

        And since then your whole life has not been
  Anything but a tribute to our doctrine.

PEER GYNT:

  Do you mean me? Peer Gynt?

OLD MAN:

              It's so unfair!
  You've kept it secret, but you've been a troll!
  The phrase I taught you was the very pole
  You climbed to make yourself a millionaire.
  Look at you, you look down your nose at me,
  But the troll credo is what you professed!

PEER GYNT:

  Enough! A mountain troll! Me? Self-obsessed?
  It's senile poppycock—it has to be!

OLD MAN *(Pulls out a bunch of old newspapers)*:

  You think we don't keep up with all the news?
  Look here—it's written down in black and white
  In the Gomorrah *Post*—it's you they choose
  To endorse; the Ronde *Times* allowed it might
  Just do the same. They thought you were a winner,
  Even before you left. Just look! They write,
  Quite truthfully I think, of how the inner
  Self is the one that counts, and that too much
  Is made of whether one can see the horn
  And tail. Written by Ida Hoof—and such
  A title—"Trolls—The Symbol of Our Nation."
  And she ends up, "Let our *enough* adorn
  The inner man!" And you're the illustration.

PEER GYNT:

  A troll? Me?

OLD MAN:

            Yes, I think they made their case.

PEER GYNT:

    I could have stayed; I didn't need to cruise
    Around the world—the Ronde was the place
    For me! I'd have saved several pairs of shoes.
    Peer Gynt—a troll? Rubbish! Delirium!
    Goodbye! You need tobacco? Take this penny.

OLD MAN:

    But—

PEER GYNT:

        Check into a sanatarium.
    You've lost your wits, old man—you haven't any!

OLD MAN:

    Exactly my intention; I accept.
    My great grandchildren, as I said before,
    Have taken over now. And furthermore,
    They're saying that I don't exist except
    In books. Well, as they say, you're only hurt by one
    You love—and nothing in my life refutes homespun
    Wisdom like that. Oh, nothing more than art—
    That's hard to swallow.

PEER GYNT:

        Yes, sir, I know what you mean.

OLD MAN:

    And I've no pension—trolls will have no part
    Of that—even a piggybank is never seen!
    The Ronde doesn't take to all that stuff.

PEER GYNT:

    No, *there* it's "To thyself be true enough!"

OLD MAN:

    Come, come! The Prince cannot complain. Our word
    Has served him well. But if he would take pity—

PEER GYNT:

    Oh, really, my dear man! Don't be absurd!

I'm strapped! Flat broke! There's nothing in the kitty,
As they say!

OLD MAN:

           No! The Prince is now a beggar, too?

PEER GYNT:

His Royal Self's in hock—as you can see!
And I have no one I can thank for that but you
Damn trolls! So—as they say—bad company . . .

OLD MAN:

Too bad! Although my hopes, at best, were tentative.
I have to go! I'm late for an audition!

PEER GYNT:

What for?

OLD MAN:

        They want someone who's representative
Of modern man and national tradition.

PEER GYNT:

Aha! Good luck—but why not mention me?
How much more contemporary can you be?
I'd like to write a farce, and call it—"A Salmagundi
Of My Experience," or "*Sic Transit Gloria Mundi.*"

(Runs down the road; the Old Man of Dovre calling after him)

At a crossroads.

PEER GYNT:

Now, more than ever, Peer, the sailing's rough;
The verdict's in on that old man's *enough*.

Your ship's gone down, so swim to open sea!
Don't—above all—get caught in the debris!
BUTTON MOLDER *(At the signpost)*:

Where is the letter of recommendation?
PEER GYNT:

So soon? I haven't had much time to look!
BUTTON MOLDER:

Oh, Peer, your face is like an open book;
It doesn't even need examination.
PEER GYNT:

I'm tired of running, and I lost my way—
BUTTON MOLDER:

And going nowhere fast, wouldn't you say?
PEER GYNT:

Well, in the woods, at night—you can go wrong!
BUTTON MOLDER:

There's an old-timer, shuffling along—
Let's call him over!
PEER GYNT:

                                No! He's drunk—dear God!

BUTTON MOLDER:

But maybe he—
PEER GYNT:

                                No, he's a little odd!

BUTTON MOLDER:

Shall we get started?
PEER GYNT:

                                First, one question—please!
"True to yourself"—what does it really mean?
BUTTON MOLDER:

My, my! I thought that you claimed expertise
In that—

PEER GYNT:

        Answer, please! Tell me what you've seen.

BUTTON MOLDER:

To be oneself, Peer Gynt, the self must die.

On you that's wasted, though, so let's confine

Ourselves to answering that one must try

To carry out the Master's grand design.

PEER GYNT:

But what if one never knew how he fit

Into the plan.

BUTTON MOLDER:

        Follow your intuition.

PEER GYNT:

If intuition isn't adequate,

What does a person do?

BUTTON MOLDER:

        Those happening

To have no intuition, Mr. Gynt,

Accompany the Hoofed One to perdition.

PEER GYNT:

This is so difficult it makes me squint!

All right, I'm not myself! My reckoning

Is I won't ever prove it, anyway.

We'll mark it down as irreclaimable;

But as you spoke, I felt a tangible

Spasm of conscience, and it made me say

Within myself: Peer, you've committed sin—

BUTTON MOLDER:

Please, not again! You don't mean to begin—

PEER GYNT:

No, this is *real*—it's not just my conceit;

I sinned indeed—in thought and word as well.

When I was overseas and raising hell—

BUTTON MOLDER:

Uh-huh! Well, could you show me a receipt?

PEER GYNT:

Sure! Give me a postponement—I'll be faster
Than lightning—I just have to find the pastor.

BUTTON MOLDER:

If you can do that, everything's all right—
You won't be melted down. But in the light
Of written orders, Peer—

PEER GYNT:

That paper's ancient;
Here, let me see—oh, yes, it's out of date.
That Peer must be insipid Peer, the merchant
Peer, who played prophet, who believed in fate!
Well, may I try?

BUTTON MOLDER:

But, Peer—!

PEER GYNT:

Please don't say no!
What do you have to do? Where will you go
That's so important? Look at that blue sky!
Smell the fresh air! A perfect place to dally—
Do you know what they say about this valley?
"No one who lives here ever wants to die!"

BUTTON MOLDER:

Till the next crossroad, Peer, and not a moment more.

PEER GYNT:

A pastor, if I have to drag one out the door!

(He runs)

————

A hillside covered with heather. A road circling around toward the top.

PEER GYNT:

 I could use *this* for almost anything,
 The man said[38] when he found the blackbird's wing.
 Who would have thought that adding up your sins
 Would be of any help right at the wire?
 A sticky situation! It begins
 To look like it's the frying pan or the fire.
 There is a proverb, though, that helps me cope
 At times like this: Where there is life, there's hope.

(A Scrawny Person in a wildly flapping cassock, with a large butterfly net over his shoulder, is running down the hill)

 What's that? A pastor brandishing a net?
 I don't—Who-eee! Am I Lady Luck's pet?
 Good evening, Pastor! My, the path is bad—
SCRAWNY PERSON:

 Of course! The things I won't do for a soul!
PEER GYNT:

 Aha! There's someone on his way to glory?
SCRAWNY PERSON:

 I hope not! I'd prefer a different story.
PEER GYNT:

 Sir, would it bother you were I to stroll
 Along?
SCRAWNY PERSON:

   Not at all—come with me, granddad.
PEER GYNT:

 I've something on my mind—

SCRAWNY PERSON:

Well! Out with it!

PEER GYNT:

You see in front of you a decent man

Who has abided by the laws; to wit,

Never done any time. Anyone can,

Of course—by fluke—not watch his step and stumble.

SCRAWNY PERSON:

Oh, yes—it's things like that that keep us humble.

PEER GYNT:

These little things—

SCRAWNY PERSON:

Just little things?

PEER GYNT:

Oh, yes,

I've stayed away from mortal sins.

SCRAWNY PERSON:

Oh, damn!

Listen to me; you'd better leave. My guess

Is I am not the one you think I am.

You're looking at my hands—what do you see?

PEER GYNT:

Some rather well-developed fingernails.

SCRAWNY PERSON:

And now you're staring at my foot? What ails

You, man?

PEER GYNT *(Pointing)*:

Is that hoof natural?

SCRAWNY PERSON:

Seems to be.

PEER GYNT *(Lifts his hat)*:

Oh, my! I could have sworn you were the pastor!

But this is better still—Forgive me, I implore;

If the front stands open, why go through another door?
Why talk to servants rather than the master?
SCRAWNY PERSON:

    You'll shake my hand? Well, isn't that nice! Dang me!
    Now please, tell me what I can do for you,
    But please don't ask for rank or revenue—
    That I can't give you even if you hang me.
    Times have been tough, you know, in my profession;
    In fact, it's nothing short of a recession.
    Souls are in short supply, both in the cradle
    And in the grave—
PEER GYNT:

                Really! You mean this generation
    Is much more virtuous?
SCRAWNY PERSON:

                  My, what imagination!
    They're worse! They end up in the casting ladle.
PEER GYNT:

    I've heard about that ladle! Actually,
    It's more or less the thing that's bothering me.
SCRAWNY PERSON:

    Speak freely!
PEER GYNT:

             If it's not an imposition,
    I'd like to have—
SCRAWNY PERSON:

                A place to stay down south?
PEER GYNT:

    You took the words, sir, right out of my mouth!
    Business is bad—right?—by your own admission,
    So maybe you could find a niche for me—
SCRAWNY PERSON:

    Dear man—

PEER GYNT:
        You don't have many applications
Surely! I wouldn't need a salary,
Merely appropriate accommodations.

SCRAWNY PERSON:
    Hmm! A warm room?

PEER GYNT:
              Not *too* warm—and the right
To come and go, certainly, as I please;
Also the understanding that I might
Move on if better opportunities—
I think that's common.

SCRAWNY PERSON:
                 I'm so sorry, friend,
But the huge quantity of comparable
Requests that I receive from honorable,
Upstanding men—you couldn't comprehend.

PEER GYNT:
    When I look back on my behavior, though,
It is a matter of entitlement!

SCRAWNY PERSON:
    Well, little things—

PEER GYNT:
              No—really decadent!
For starters, I was in the slave trade!

SCRAWNY PERSON:
             Oh,
Others have traded wills and minds—not well
Enough, though, to get in.

PEER GYNT:
             I sent some Brahman
Idols to China.

SCRAWNY PERSON:

                         Please! That is so common
        You would be teased and heckled. Let me tell
        You there are many people who put even worse
        Idols in sermons, literature—especially verse—
        And even they must stand in line.

PEER GYNT:

                              But I
        Pretended once to be a prophet!

SCRAWNY PERSON:

                              You?
        Abroad? Pshaw! A man who flies too high
        Will fall flat on his face, friend, en route to
        The melting spoon. If you have nothing more
        Than that, you'll never get beyond the door.

PEER GYNT:

        I once was shipwrecked—not so far away—
        They say a drowning man will grab a straw—
        Look out for number one, they also say—
        Well I sort of—halfway—well, broke the law
        And let the cook go down.

SCRAWNY PERSON:

                         I might accept
        A halfway pregnant cooking girl; except
        What is this "sort of, halfway" jibber-jabber
        Anyway? Really, who would pay a decent wage
        Or burn expensive fuel—in this day and age—
        To warm up such a nauseating clabber?
        I'm sorry, but your sins are barely worth
        Contempt; in plain words, sir—your time on earth
        Was wasted; you must play a different tune—
        Resign yourself now to the melting spoon.
        Besides, were I to give you room and board,

What would you gain? It wouldn't be a boon.
You'd keep your memory, but what reward
Would that entail, since what you have to view—
The landscape of your soul—would soon make you,
As Englishmen would say, just too, too bored.
Nothing that would depress or stimulate you—
No cause for celebration or despair;
There's nothing cold or hot, but everywhere
You look you'll find something to irritate you.

PEER GYNT:

I've seen it written—quite convincingly—
That no one knows where my shoe pinches me.

SCRAWNY PERSON:

That's true. I, of course—thanks to You Know Who—
Need fret about only a single shoe.
You mentioned shoes, and that reminds me that
I really must be going—I almost
Forgot—I'm to pick up a juicy roast.
I'm sorry, but I don't have time to chat—.

PEER GYNT:

If you don't mind my asking, what's the grain
This sinner fed upon?

SCRAWNY PERSON:

                    All I hear say
Is that he was himself, both night and day,
Which, of course, puts him under our domain.

PEER GYNT:

Himself? Does *that* kind wash up on your shore?

SCRAWNY PERSON:

Sometimes. At least they've one foot in the door.
You are yourself, you know, in different ways—
You can be right side out or wrong side out,
Just like a coat. While puttering about

In Paris, someone found that the sun's rays
Can etch a portrait, with a quality
That's true to life, or in the negative,
So-called, in which shadow and light will be
Reversed. For some, that's not evocative,
But the facsimile is there as well
And with appropriate materiel
Will be revealed. Now let us say a soul
Is photographed in negative. The plate
Is not therefore considered second-rate—
It's sent to me, put through the rigmarole
Of further treatment and development
Until at last an obvious change takes place.
After I steam and dip and burn each face
With sulphur or a like ingredient,
The form appears the way it was intended—
In other words, what's called the positive.
But if—like you—the soul's been unattended,
Sulphur nor lye nor any fixative
Can do the job.

PEER GYNT:

                    One arrives black—a crow—
But becomes white—a dove—to coin a phrase.
Who's in this negative that will amaze
Us so in positive—or don't you know?

SCRAWNY PERSON:

It's Peter Gynt.

PEER GYNT:

                Peter Gynt—is that so?
Is Mr. Gynt himself?

SCRAWNY PERSON:

                He swears he is.

PEER GYNT:
    I'm sure he has the best of references.
SCRAWNY PERSON:
    You know him?
PEER GYNT:
                        Oh, I think so, but—you know—
    One knows so many people.
SCRAWNY PERSON:
                        Time is short—
    Where did you see him last?
PEER GYNT:
                        Around the Cape.
SCRAWNY PERSON:
    Buona Speranza?
PEER GYNT:
                        Yes, at last report,
    But he'll set sail once everything's shipshape.
SCRAWNY PERSON:
    Then I must get down there immediately.
    This almost makes me want to call it quits!
    The Cape is not a happy place for me—
    It's full of missionaries—Jesuits!

    (He runs in a southerly direction)

PEER GYNT:
    The greedy pig! Look at him running off,
    Tongue hanging out! Ha! Won't his face be red!
    Dumb as an ass! Forgive me if I scoff,
    But what conceit! He should have been misled!
    I don't know what makes him so arrogant.
    As far as clients go, he's indigent!
    It won't be long before he falls right off

His high horse. But I guess *my* saddle's slipping, too;
The club of *self* says I'm someone they never knew!

(A shooting star, barely visible; he nods to it)

A shooting star! Greetings, my brother in the sky!
We shine, we flare, we fall, all in the blink of an eye—

(He slumps in anguish, and walks deeper into the mist; quiet for a moment, then he screams)

Is there no one, no one upon this teeming earth—
Is there no one below, is there no one above!

(Appears farther downhill, throws his hat in the road and pulls his hair. After a while, a stillness comes over him)

In such dire poverty do souls finally shove
Off into nothingness—without a thing of worth.
Beautiful earth, tell me how to repay
My trampling upon your grass in vain?
Beautiful sun, why did you fritter away
Your rays on uninhabited domain?
No one to warm, no voices in the air—
The owner, so they say, was never there.
Beautiful sun, and oh, you beautiful earth
Why did you bear my mother? Why did you light her way?
The spirit's mean, but nature's profligate, I'd say!
Life is too high a price to pay for birth.
I want to climb—high up! I want to climb
A peak and see the sunrise one more time,
Stare till I'm weary at the promised land,
And let them then pile snow upon my bier
And write above my head, "*No one* lies here."
And then, thereafter—when I'm gone and—and—
Ah, who gives a damn!

CHURCHGOERS *(Singing on the forest path)*:
>   Oh, what a blessed morn
>   When tongues of glory
>   Strike the earth like a flaming sword.
>   Children of God are born
>   Singing His story
>   With the glorious tongue of the Lord.

PEER GYNT *(Recoils in terror)*:
>   Don't look! It's waste and desert on the other side.
>   I fear that I was dead long, long before I died.

(Tries to hide behind some bushes, but finds himself at a crossroads)

BUTTON MOLDER:
>   Good morning, Peer! Did you find your receipt?

PEER GYNT:
>   I sifted through my autobiography
>   To no avail.

BUTTON MOLDER:
>   You found nothing concrete?

PEER GYNT:
>   Only a lesson in photography.

BUTTON MOLDER:
>   It's time! Your troubles now are through.

PEER GYNT:
>   Everything's through.
>   The owl can smell a rat—hear his tu-whit tu-whoo?

BUTTON MOLDER:
>   No, that's the church bell.

PEER GYNT *(Points)*:
>   What's that shining over there?

BUTTON MOLDER:
>   Only a cabin light.

PEER GYNT:

What is that hollow sound?

BUTTON MOLDER:

A woman singing.

PEER GYNT:

There's no need to run around—
There's my receipt.

BUTTON MOLDER *(Grabbing him)*:

Please put your house in order, Peer!

(They emerge from the grove of trees and stand beside the cabin. Daybreak)

PEER GYNT:

Put it in order? There it is! Behold!
Now go! Get out of here! Had your spoon been
Big as a coffin, still it could not hold
Me and my sins!

BUTTON MOLDER:

Till the third crossroad, *then*—!

(He turns away and leaves)

PEER GYNT *(Approaches the cabin)*:

It's just as far, forward or back;
Outside or in looks just as black!

(Stops)

No! To go in, go home, to make amends
Would be an agony that never ends!

(Takes a few steps; but stops again)

Go 'round, the Great Between said!

(Hears singing in the cabin)

Yes, but not
This time! I'm going through no matter what!

(He runs toward the house; at the same time, Solveig comes out the door, dressed for church, with a prayerbook in her hand; she holds a walking stick in the other. She stands erect, with a gentle expression)

PEER GYNT *(Throwing himself down at the threshold)*:
Punish a sinner—shout it out—shout it out loud!
SOLVEIG:
He's here! Praise be to God! He's here—just as he vowed!

(Fumbling for him)

PEER GYNT:
Shout out the many sins I have committed!
SOLVEIG:
In nothing have you sinned—I have acquitted
You, my boy!

(Fumbles for him again and finds him)

BUTTON MOLDER *(Behind the cabin)*:
Your receipt!
PEER GYNT:
Shout my iniquity!
SOLVEIG *(Sits next to him)*:
You made my life into a never-ending song.
Blessed be this dawn that brings you home where you
belong,
And blessed be my boy for coming back to me!
PEER GYNT:
I'm lost!
SOLVEIG:
But He will listen to your prayer.

PEER GYNT *(Laughs)*:

    Lost! Unless you solve riddles!

SOLVEIG:

Let me try.

PEER GYNT:

    Let you try? Sure—why not? Can you say where
    Peer Gynt has been since last we said goodbye?

SOLVEIG:

    Been?

PEER GYNT:

How has he fulfilled his destiny—

    The one he's marked with in the eyes of God?
    Can you tell me? If not, my home will be
    The mist—wandering in the Land of Nod.

SOLVEIG *(Smiles)*:

    Oh, yes, I know the answer.

PEER GYNT:

Tell it to me!

    Where have I been myself, wholly and truly,
    Made manifest the sign of God above?

SOLVEIG:

    Here—in my faith, my hope, and in my love.

PEER GYNT *(Recoils in surprise)*:

    Stop it! You're talking nonsense—it's untrue!
    You are the mother of that boy in there!

SOLVEIG:

    I am—but who's the father, Peer? He who
    Forgives in answer to a mother's prayer.

PEER GYNT *(Bathed in a ray of light, he screams)*:

    Innocent woman—my mother and my bride!
    Oh, hide me, Solveig, hide me there inside!

(He clings to her and hides his face in her lap. A long silence. The sun rises)

SOLVEIG *(Singing softly)*:
> Sleep now, my sweetest boy!
> I will watch over you and rock you.

> The mother and her boy will play and play.
> Oh, they have played away the livelong day.

> The mother's breast was longing for her boy
> The livelong day. God give you peace and joy!

> The mother and her boy were heart to heart
> The livelong day. Now they will never part.

> Sleep now, my sweetest boy!
> I will watch over you and rock you.

BUTTON MOLDER'S VOICE *(Behind the cabin)*:
> Till the next crossroad, Peer, and *then* the score
> Has to be settled. Now, I'll say no more.

SOLVEIG *(Sings louder as the sun grows brighter)*:
> I will watch over you and rock you;
> Sleep and dream, my sweetest boy!

THE END

Notes

1. Ibsen published *Peer Gynt* in 1867. He was, therefore, referring to the turn of the nineteenth century.

2. The largest of all the valleys in Eastern Norway.

3. Pronounced "pair."

4. Gjendin ridge is thought to be a precipitous mountain ridge near Lake Gjende, which is actually named Besseggen.

5. Pronounced "GŪD-brahnd GLĔSS-neh"—a character from Asbjornsen and Moe, well-known mid-nineteenth century collectors of folk tales; like Peer, the character was based on a real person.

6. Pronounced "MAHDS MOO-un."

7. Pronounced "AW-suh."

8. A typical Norwegian farm would have had several buildings— one the parlor room, one the dining room, one the kitchen, etc., as well as outbuildings for the animals and grain.

9. Pronounced "Hay-DOLL-en", now called Heidal, a valley near Gudbrandsdal.

10. An alcoholic brew about 80 proof, made on the farm—the homemade predecessor to aquavit; literally, burning wine.

11. Pronounced "TRAWND, KOR-uh, and BOARD."

12. Refers to the Rondane Mountains, located to the east of Gudbrandsdalen.

13. "Boar's head" in German.

14. "Trumpet blast" in Swedish.

15. An idiomatic Swedish expression meaning roughly, "Shame on you."

16. King of Sweden from 1660-1697, involved in many battles.

17. Usually Bendery, a city in what is now western Russia where Charles XII laid siege to Turkish troops.

18. Charles XII is said to have used his spurs to tear the Sultan's robe in a fit of rage. The "famous" bucklers for the spurs were lost.

19. A Turkish soldier.

20. A misquotation of the Goethe line from *Faust* meaning, "The eternal feminine leads us on." The correct line is "zieht uns hinan" meaning "leads us upward."

21. Lyrics are tailored for the Grieg music. They are more concise in Ibsen's manuscript, as follows:
    Winter and spring will disappear
    And summer, too—even a year.
    But one day you'll return to me, I know.
    I'm waiting—as I promised long ago.

God give you strength if you are all alone!
God bless you if you stand before His throne!
Here I will wait 'til you return, my friend.
If you're with God, I'll join you in the end.

22. A colossal statue near Thebes said to produce a musical sound when the rays of the early morning sun strike it.

23. Past participle of the German verb "to understand."

24. A question of vital importance.

25. A reference to the Septuagint, the oldest Greek version of the Old Testament, traditionally said to have been translated by 70 Jewish scholars at the request of Ptolemy II.

The subsequent "one hundred sixty" is presumably the number of inmates in the asylum.

26. Mikkel is a name associated with foxes (a la Felix the Cat) in Norwegian, Schlingel is "rascal" in German (Norwegian is slyngel), and Schaf is "sheep" in German and Fox was Fuchs in the original, German for "fox."

27. Baron von Munchhausen (1720-97), a German soldier and adventurer, and—more important—a teller of tall tales.

28. "Right" and "left" in German.

29. "Long live the great Peer!"

30. Pronounced YŌK-ul. All the names are of glaciers and peaks in western Norway, although not all could be seen at once as Ibsen has it.

31. Pronounced FOAL-guh-FUN.

32. Pronounced BLAW-hu.

33. Pronounced GAL-doe-PIG-gun. The highest mountain in Norway, located in Jotanheimen.

34. Pronounced Hore-TAY-gun.

35. Glittertinden is also a peak in western Norway.

36. Thought to be a reference to another tale by the famous Asbjornsen and Moe.

37. Loosely translated: "A man must cover himself."

38. Literally, "As Esben said"—a reference to a Norwegian fairy tale in which Esben Askeladd finds a blackbird's wing, which seems to be useless, but in the end enables him to marry the princess and live happily ever after.

THE PLAYS OF HENRIK IBSEN

1849
Cataline

1849–50
The Warrior's Barrow

1851
Norma

1852
St. John's Eve

1854
Lady Inger of Östraat

1855
The Feast at Solhaug

1856
Olaf Liljekrans

1857
The Vikings at Helgeland

1862
Love's Comedy

1863
The Pretenders

1865
Brand

1867
Peer Gynt

1868–69
The League of Youth

1864–73
Emperor and Galilean

1875–77
The Pillars of Society

1879
A Doll House

1881
Ghosts

1882
An Enemy of the People

1884
The Wild Duck

1886
Rosmersholm

1888
The Lady from the Sea

1890
Hedda Gabler

1892
The Master Builder

1894
Little Eyolf

1896
John Gabriel Borkman

1899
When We Dead Awaken

THE PLAYWRIGHT

HENRIK IBSEN was born in 1828 in the small town of Skien, Norway. His father, Knud Ibsen, owned a general store, but while Henrik was still a young boy, the family encountered financial distress from which they did not recover. As a consequence, Henrik began working full-time in a pharmacy before he was 16. At 18 he fathered a child out-of-wedlock, whom he was to support for 14 years. In 1849, stealing hours at night, he wrote his first play, *Catiline*. In 1850, at age 22, he entered the university in Christiania (now called Oslo), continuing to write plays; but a year later, he was offered a beginning position at the Bergen Theater which he immediately accepted. He would spend six years there, writing and directing, before moving on to the directorship of the Norwegian Theater of Christiania, which he led until it failed in 1862.

In 1864, Ibsen began a period of self-imposed exile in Italy and Germany that was to last 27 years, during which he would write almost all his best-known plays, beginning with *Brand* and *Peer Gynt*, then moving on to the great works in prose. It was not until 1891 that he would return to reside in Norway—a celebrated author—where he remained until his death in 1906.

THE TRANSLATORS

GERRY BAMMAN wrote *A Thousand Nights And A Night*, a musical adaptation of the Arabian Nights, which was produced in New York in 1977. His play *Ecco!* won the CBS/Dramatists Guild National Residency Award in 1983. He has also written *Remember Chowchilla!*, a cartoon fantasy about an actor becoming president, and several film scripts in which politicians are actors. He has performed, taught and directed in theatre, film and television throughout the United States, Canada and Europe.

IRENE B. BERMAN, a native of Oslo, Norway, was educated in Norway and Switzerland before moving to America. Ms. Berman owns and operates Accent, Inc., a translation agency in West Hartford, Connecticut, which handles linguistic services in more than 30 languages. In addition, she works nationally as a freelance translator and interpreter of Scandinavian languages.

The Bamman/Berman translations of Ibsen's *A Doll House*, *Hedda Gabler*, *The Master Builder*, *The Wild Duck* and *Peer Gynt* have received productions at Hartford Stage Company, La Jolla Playhouse, Los Angeles Theatre Center, Berkeley Repertory Theatre and Arena Stage.